Reviews

A rare find of the twenty-first century "How to Maximize Your Professional Performance and Productivity" is refreshing, honest, and all-encompassing. Calvin Dickens captures in one work the mechanics and soft skills necessary to maneuver the complicated landscape of professional life in the twenty-first century and beyond. He explores the brilliance and simplicity, the intricate balance that must be judiciously applied to matters of family, faith, and function (how we choose to earn a living). It is a must read for professionals who aspire to be the best they can possibly be.

Denise Kelly

Aerospace and program management consultant

and entrepreneur

Calvin Dickens is an insightful and trusted adviser to individuals and organizations interested in improving their performance in the professional work environment. He has just finished his first book in the form of a guide, providing for his readers practical principles and viewpoints. This guide is very concise and gets to the heart of the subject quickly. It uses easy and understandable terms that will help you think clearly about the power of organizational and business development. Publicly I say, "Calvin, this project is truly a blessing!"

Professor Robert Simms

Retired educator and developer of the Simms Method

Simmsmethod.com

Calvin Dickens has finally done what all the textbooks, business professionals, so-called experts, and professors have not been able to do: he has written a concise guide in plain, easy-to-follow English on the maximization of performance and productivity. I have been in aviation for fifteen years and a university instructor for two years, and I can say that this book is dead on. It's a must-read for every high school senior that has dreams of going to college, every undergraduate student, graduate student, and working professional. This book is packed with facts, not fluff. The illustrations are simple yet mind blowing. Everyone who reads this guide will be able to relate to it; Calvin just finally put it on paper. If you plan on going to the top, taking yourself to that next level, this is a must-read.

H. Randle III
Instructor of aviation, Florida Memorial University

Just imagine if my generation, coming out of college fifteen or twenty years ago, had a chance to experience the information within this book. I believe we would have been more productive, more humble, and more considerate. It would have prevented many workplace hiccups. I call this book the 10 Mental Toughness Secrets of the Corporate Workforce. A must-read, I must say!

Tasjah D. Hall
Aviation consultant and entrepreneur

A must-read for any young professional that wants to know how to gain an advantage. Calvin does an excellent job of providing insight on the dos and don'ts for everyone looking to advance their career.

Steve Caldwell
IT director, Higher Dimension Church

By

C. E. Dickens

(Aspiring Professionals)
How To Enhance Your Professional Performance and Productivity

When facing workplace obstacles, learn practical insights that will enable you to recognize, strategize, and ultimately experience success!

Copyright © 2013 C. E. Dickens

All rights reserved.

ISBN-10: 1482030357

EAN-13: 9781482030358

Library of Congress Control Number: 2013901420
CreateSpace Independent Publishing Platform
North Charleston, South Carolina

Aggrandizing Your Personal Operating System

What happens when you face workplace obstacles?

Do you yearn to learn practical insights that will enable you to recognize and strategize how to overcome workplace obstacles?

Do you want to experience success?

Dedication

To my late mother, Ora M. Peterson, who above all taught me sacrifice, commitment, integrity, hard work, and the importance of faith. I am thankful to her for also playing the role of father, motivating me to lead, protect and provide for my children.

To my wife, Fanetta, who taught me the meaning of true love, giving, and trusting.

To my daughters, Camile and Latrice, who taught me vulnerability, gentleness, and happiness.

*And to my pastor,
Pastor "J," for his remarkable spiritual insight and his gift of encouraging others to pursue the entrepreneurial spirit within us.*

Special Thanks

Special thanks to T. Hall, H. Randle, C. Watkins, R. Ramoutar, J. Nwambuonno, and M. Hall for inspiring me by unknowingly encouraging me to share with others what I privately shared with you. It is through my relationships with each of you that I was able to test my "aggrandizing" concepts with a group of the youngest and brightest the aviation industry has to offer.

Table of Contents

Chapter	Page
Foreword	xiii
The Operating System Concept Defined	1
Let's Clear the Air About Professionalism, Performance, and Productivity	5
Significance of the Ten Operating Systems	11
Chapter 1 - The "Develop Self-Discipline" Operating System	15
Chapter 2 - The "Be Trustworthy" Operating System	29
Chapter 3 - The "Exercise Honesty and Integrity" Operating System	41
Chapter 4 - The "Practice Fairness and Consistency" Operating System	51
Chapter 5 - The "Maintain a Positive Outlook" Operating System	65
Chapter 6 - The "Personal and Professional Development" Operating System	79
Chapter 7 - The "Strive for Excellence" Operating System	97
Chapter 8 - The "Embrace Technology" Operating System	117
Chapter 9 - The "Be Adaptable to Change" Operating System	131
Chapter 10 - The "Faith and Divine Authority" Operating System	145
Bonus Module—A Snippet on Leadership	159
That's a Wrap	163
About the Author	165
Resources	167

Illustrations

	Page
Computer Operating System (Illustrated)	3
The "Aggrandizing Your Personal Operating System (Diagram)	9
E^5 Theory	113
The Action Gap	115
Generations and Their Characteristics	141

Foreword

Congratulations! You've got that degree. You obtained that certification. You finished your military commitment. You have just landed or are about to land that all-important job. What next?

How do you navigate your way through the next phase of your budding career? How do you transfer your hard-earned classroom skills or military training into becoming a productive and well-rounded employee? What challenges lie ahead? What are the expectations? How do you get along with a difficult boss? Are there any workplace-related complexities that you need to be aware of, such as understanding "influential" power and authority? Will there be a lot of changes? How should you dress? Do you know how to do an implied task? In preparing to make the transition into the professional work environment, have you overlooked anything?

This book is designed to give you some insight into how to manage these concerns.

I have discovered there is a great need for personal and professional development. For many who are entering into the workplace environment for the first time, the need for personal and professional development extends to mentoring; learning to be the best you can be, making personal assessments, mastering professional relationships, and maneuvering in and around workplace politics. This project condenses all my knowledge and experiences into what I believe is a one-stop "winning formula" that will enable you to learn how to operate very well in a work environment.

This is not a book about leadership. Books about leadership can be found in every nook and cranny known to man. Rather than focusing on managing or leading others, this book is about managing and leading yourself while in a work environment. It provides practical principles and viewpoints to help guide you through challenges as you attempt to navigate your way through the professional work environment.

My goal is to help you, whether you are transitioning into the workforce after college, helping those who are transitioning into a professional environment after completing a certification, leaving the military, or simply looking to enhance yourself personally or professionally.

(Aspiring Professionals) How to Enhance Your Professional Performance and Productivity

View from the Top of Pinnacle Peak—Mount Rainer, Washington
Credit: wallpaper5.com

A pinnacle is the highest or topmost point or level of something. It is a lofty peak or the highest point. It is success, power, and fame. If you are on top of your career, you have reached the pinnacle.

The above photograph and definition is a metaphorical reflection on achieving success in your career, emphasizing how you must climb (work) to get to the top. You cannot get to the top alone. The climb (work) requires resources, strategies, and a plan. *How To Enhance Your Professional Performance and Productivity* is designed to be a tool to assist you as you start your climb. Once there, the reward is a view that is simply breathtaking, exhilarating, and rewarding. However, once you have arrived at the pinnacle, you can't rest on your laurels. You must begin anchoring yourself; after all, the winds can blow pretty hard when you are standing at the pinnacle.

Note: A photograph of almost any other peak would have been sufficient to illustrate the point being made here, but this view was so spectacular. For several years, I lived and worked every day with a full view of this magnificent mountain range.

The Operating System Concept Defined

The operating system is the most important program on a computer. Every computer must have an operating system to run other programs. Operating systems perform basic tasks, such as recognizing input from the keyboard, sending output to the display screen, keeping track of files and directories on disks, and controlling peripheral devices such as disk drives and printers. (See the illustration on page 3)

Operating systems provide a software platform on top of which other programs, called application programs, can run. The application programs must be written to run on top of a particular operating system. Therefore, your choice of an operating system determines the applications you can run. For PCs, the most popular operating systems are DOS, OS/2, and Windows, but others are available, such as Linux.

Those things in life that shape who we are as a person are our personal operating systems. They shape who we are and include our environment, attitude, values, beliefs, characteristics, and traits; the level of our ambition, commitment, dedication; our socioeconomic backgrounds; and other criteria and influences.

This project is designed like a computer operating system. The most important program helps to shape us and determines how we prosper. To prosper in the workplace or to focus on maximizing our professional performance and production, we use our personal operating system, just as a computer uses its operating system. Your personal operating system, along with the operating systems presented in this book, are the foundational source to catapult you to maximizing your professional performance and productivity.

I searched all available resources, over and over, in an attempt to capture a single word that would reveal exactly what I am trying to convey in regard to combining all operating system components. I stumbled on a word I had never used and seldom heard: *aggrandize*. It means to increase or improve the power, wealth, influence, or status of somebody or something, especially by a deliberate plan (enlarge, increase, enhance). Suddenly the light came on! By publishing this project, my goal is to help individuals aggrandize their personal operating systems.

The *How to Enhance Your Professional Performance and Productivity* contains ten chapters. There are ten numbers on a keyboard. A combination of numbers can create other numbers, totals, and figures. Just like the numbers on a keyboard, the ten chapters can be used in various combinations to help illustrate or create solutions, outcomes, and successes. Also like the numbers on a keyboard, the potential combinations are endless, and so it is with the Aggrandizing Your Personal Operating System; the potential combinations and solutions are endless. I believe that all attributes and traits impacting your ability to maximize your professional performance and productivity are based on what we have coined as our ten core modules.

Computer Operating System
(Illustrated)

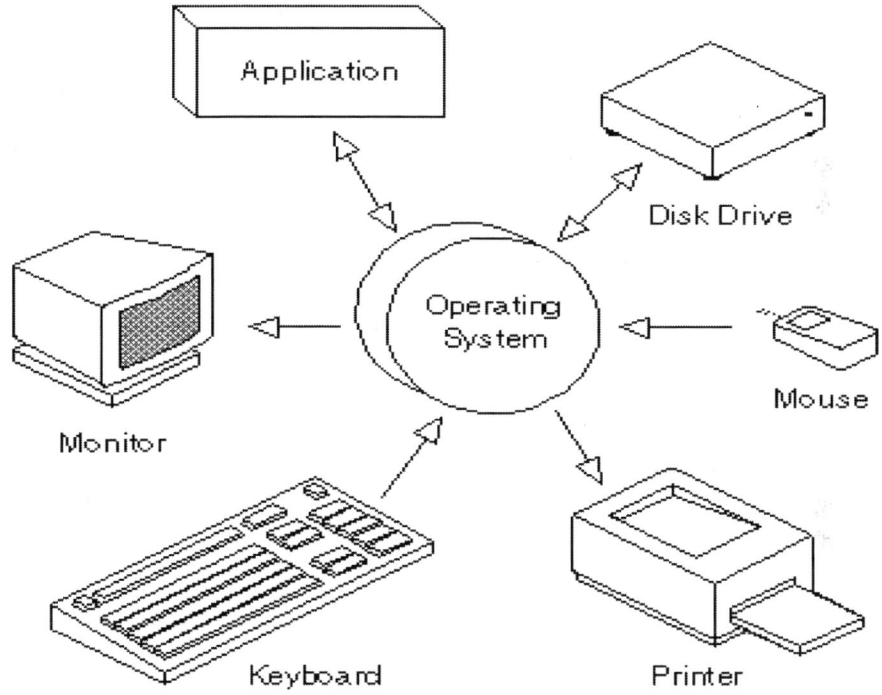

Like the computer operating system shown above, each of the ten chapters in this book has a central theme. Each theme is supported by surrounding application programs—that is, essential professional or personal attributes that are independently explored.

Let's Clear the Air about Professionalism, Performance, and Productivity

I don't want to start this journey with the assumption that everybody fully understands the true significance and meaning of the three principle words in the title: *professionalism*, *performance*, and *productivity*. To clarify, I want to explore on the true meaning of these words before we go any further.

Professionalism

The guidelines describing how to be a professional give ample consideration to how employees dress and conduct themselves. Employees are expected to be respectful, polite, well mannered, considerate, and understanding while interacting with fellow employees, internal and external customers, tenants, concessionaires, and contractors. Professional considerations also extend to e-mails, messages, faxes, and phone calls. Professionalism requires everyone to use appropriate business terms while speaking in the workplace.

Knowing the right things and delivering the correct information to others is also part of professionalism.

Professionalism means employees are doing their job with sincerity and competence while maintaining etiquette and ethics in the workplace. Professionalism leads to logical and unbiased decision making, making it the basis for a good work environment. Professionalism is important in the workplace because it

- maintains a certain standard of conduct and performance by all;
- promotes good team spirit;
- helps encourage employees to remain motivated;
- ensures fairness;
- maintains the proper communications flow in the workplace;
- enables your company or organization to achieve its stated goals; and
- protects, promotes, and produces the company or organization's brand.

A lack of professionalism produces

- a lack of motivation;
- a lack of employee ownership;
- unethical acts that mar the company's or organization's reputation;
- a higher attrition rate, which keeps the company's or organization's hiring process in perpetual motion, creating a strain on the company or organization;
- a lack of loyalty between management and employees; and
- possible litigation.

Professionalism is the axis around which the company or organization revolves. Without this axis, the organization is like a ship without a rudder. More importantly, professionalism begins and ends with each individual member of the company or organization.

Performance

Performance is what is expected of you while on the job on a day-to-day basis. *Performance* can further be defined as adhering to an expected standard. Typically, when the word *performance* is associated with the workplace, it is accompanied with an adjective, such as *high*, *low*, *outstanding*, or *professional*. Your performance is the way in which you do a job, how effective you are, or how you carry out or accomplish something.

Your performance is an integral component of the way others see you on the job. Your employee evaluation is based on subjective and measurable assessments of your performance. Everyone on the job is evaluated based on their performance; *everyone*, from the chief executive officer all the way to the most recently hired entry-level worker, is evaluated based on his or her performance. Your performance is your personal contributions toward helping the company or organization achieve its goal or mission. Performance is usually viewed differently by supervisors and employees.

Your performance can be affected by a plethora of factors. What occurs away from the job can also have a major impact on your performance. In fact, every module mentioned in this book can affect your performance. And here is one thing that's certain: your performance is just that—yours. You and you alone assume direct responsibility for high, average, low, or even substandard performance.

Productivity

What causes low productivity among employees? It can be a number of things. Employees are individuals, and the things that affect them negatively in the workplace are unique. They can be poorly matched to a job in which they don't have the skills to be successful. Or the employee may have a poor work ethic, extreme job dissatisfaction, a lack of training, a lack of resources, or difficulty with a bad manager. Whatever the factors may be, each company or organization must understand how to identify the root of the problem and how it relates to low productivity so that strategies can be established to improve productivity.

So, how can you improve employee productivity within a company or organization? Increases in productivity can be achieved by knowing more about employees and what motivates them. Managers must find ways to understand what drives each individual employee within the context of his or her respective roles in the workplace. Every employee has a different reason for working. Some may be motivated by things like performance-based bonuses, opportunities for promotion, benefits, personal satisfaction, flexible working conditions, or additional paid time off. Others work to accomplish goals and to feel as if they are contributing to something larger than themselves. Whatever their reasons may be, employees must find satisfaction in their work, or they may become unhappy and unproductive.

Many companies or organizations use job satisfaction surveys to help find ways to motivate employees as individuals. By using job satisfaction surveys, managers are able to find out what makes employees want to live up to their full potential.

Well-thought-out job descriptions and performance appraisals can be used to match people with the kind of work they like to do. Employee productivity can also be enhanced by measuring the factors that mark the difference between success and failure in specific jobs, by placing the right person in the right position, by allowing each employee to utilize his or her talents without limitations. This leads to greater job satisfaction and improved morale, because the company or organization is staffed with a workforce of people who are highly productive, skilled, and committed to doing their very best.

The role of management is to ensure that the necessary resources are available to ensure productivity. The resources for this include proper training, equipment, personnel, and proven processes. Once these resources are made available, it's up to the individual employee and his or her team to produce or execute the desired outcome. The desired outcome results in increased productivity. Desired productivity levels are a shared responsibility between the individual employee, his or her team, and management.

If something in the workplace is lacking, it is up to the individual employee, his or her team, or management to identify and provide the missing link or element.

The "Aggrandizing Your Personal Operating System" Module (Diagram)

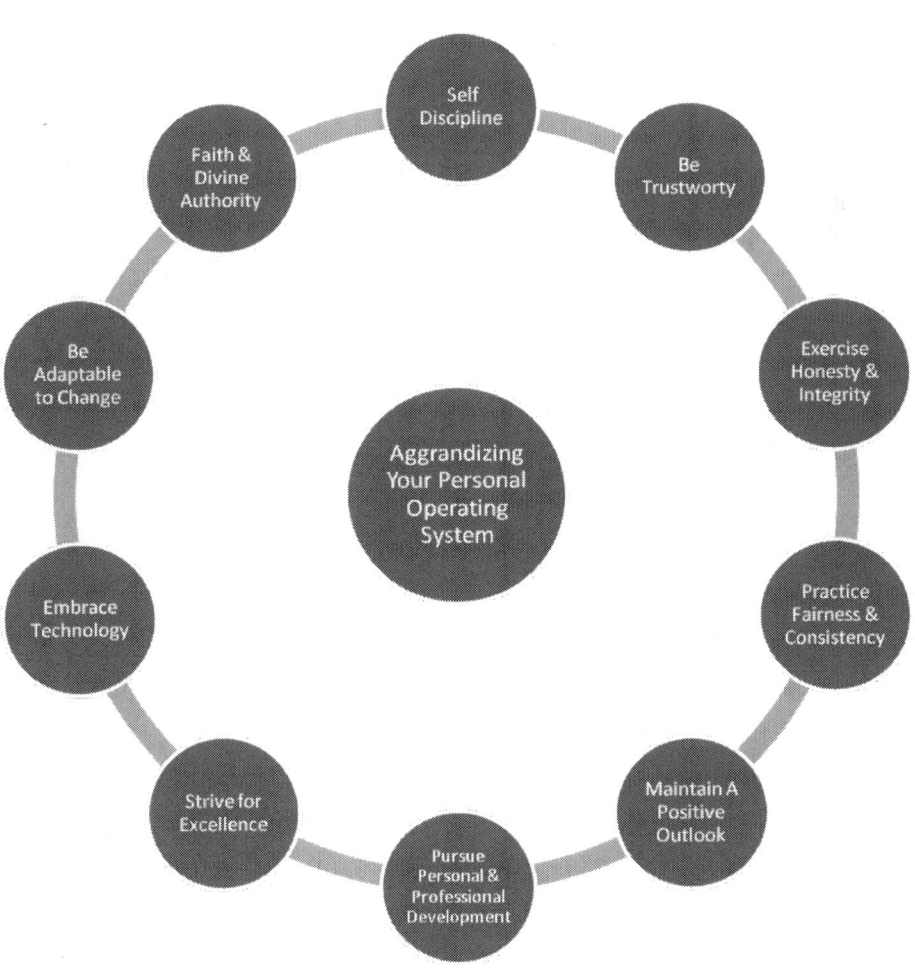

The Significance of the Ten Chapters

Let me take a moment to discuss my thinking behind the concepts in the ten chapters that make up the Aggrandizing Your Personal Operating System.

As a person of faith, I believe that the Creator created humans. We are distinct from the rest of creation. The divine Triune Council determined that we were to have God's image and likeness. We are spiritual beings who are not only body, but also soul and spirit. The human is a moral being whose intelligence, perception, and self-determination far exceed that of any other earthly being.

Capacity and ability require accountability and responsibility. We should never be pleased to dwell on a level of existence lower than the one God has made possible for us. *We should strive to be the best we can be and to reach the highest levels we can reach.* To do less would make us unfaithful stewards of the life entrusted to us.

Aggrandizing Your Personal Operating System reflects the Creator and us. Ten chapters were selected based on the central theme, "Aggrandizing Your Personal Operating System," to represent wholeness and completeness. There are non-biblical and biblical symbols that represent the number ten—these same symbols reflect the ten core modules.

Non-biblical Symbolism of the Number Ten

- 10 is a symbol of *harmony:* 4 + 6.

- For Pythagoras (one of the most famous and controversial ancient Greek philosophers, who lived from about 570 to about 490 BCE), 10 was the symbol of the universe, and it also expressed the *whole of human knowledge.*

- The number 10 is regarded as the *most perfect* of numbers, because it contains the unit that did it all and zero, the symbol of the matter and chaos, from which all came about. Therefore, it includes in its figure the created and the non-created, the beginning and the end, the power and the force, the life and the nothing.

- It represents *straightness in the faith,* because it is the first number "in extension" (of two digits), just as a hundred and a thousand, explains Hugh of Saint-Victor.

- According to Heinrich Cornelius Agrippa (a German magician, occult writer, theologian, astrologer, and alchemist), "Ten is called the number of all or universal, and the complete number marking the full course of life." He attributes to it a *sense of totality,* of achievement, the return to the unit after the development of the cycle of the first nine numbers.

- According to the Mayas (a Native American people of Central America and southern Mexico whose classical culture flourished between the fourth and the eighth centuries AD), it represents *the end of a cycle and the beginning of another.* Ten was regarded as being the number of life and of death.

- In China, the cross represents the number ten—as the totality of the numbers.

- *Ten is the remains of goodness and truth.* Emanuel Swedenborg, a Swedish scientist, philosopher, Christian mystic, and theologian, used the word *remains* to denote feelings of love and goodness and true ideas that are stored up in the inner person from earliest childhood for use later in life. Ten is a sufficient amount of goodness and truth joined together: 10=5x2.

Biblical Symbolism of the Number Ten

- Ten represents the *Creator* and the *creation*—3 + 7—the Trinity resting in the expressed universe.

- There are *ten* I AMs of Jesus in the Gospel according to John.

- The Ten Commandments of Exodus 20:2-13 and Deuteronomy 5:6-17 are considered a *cornerstone* of Judaism and Christianity.

- People traditionally tithed one-tenth of their produce. The tithe *represents the whole* of what was due to God; it marks and recognizes God's claim on the whole.

- The Lord's Prayer is completed in *ten* clauses.

- The Bible records ten generations between Adam and Noah, and ten generations between Noah and Abraham

- The ten plagues represent the *complete* circle of God's judgments on Egypt. (Exodus 9:14 says, "I will . . . send all my plagues.")

- The number 10 represents revelation and divine law.

- Abraham's faith was provided by a completed cycle of ten trials.

- God promised not to destroy Sodom and Gomorrah if only 10 righteous people can be found in them.

- There were 10 witnesses supporting Boaz to marry Ruth.

- **The Tenth Generation** - The tenth generation completed and represented the whole existence of the family or nation.

As we recognize non-biblical and biblical symbolism that reflect the number ten, we can see that ten is symbolic of whole, perfect, straightness, all, totality, goodness and truth, that Creator and creation, the divine, and the deliverer. By the time you finish reading and applying the ten chapters of *How To Enhance Your Professional Performance and Productivity*, it is my hope that you to will be able to discover the wholeness and true meaning of what's in store for you as you use the Aggrandizing Your Personal Operating System to maximize your professional performance and productivity.

The "Develop Self-Discipline" Operating System

The "Develop Self-Discipline" Operating System

While aligning the ten modules for this publication, I purposely placed the self-discipline module first. I did this to reinforce the idea that having self-discipline is the foundation that everything else in our lives is built on or revolves around. Everything you do in life requires self-discipline, such as being a student. What happens when you fail

> *Self-discipline is the willpower and self-control to do the right thing when no one is looking.*

to study for that next exam? Being a business professional requires self-discipline; what happens if you procrastinate and fail to complete a project by its due date? Having a good time with friends requires self-discipline; what risks do you take if you get into an automobile with a driver who has obviously been drinking? These examples illustrate the importance of self-discipline, which enables you to make sound decisions.

A lack of self-discipline will greatly impact your personal as well as your professional performance and productivity. Having self-discipline is more important and more difficult than having physical prowess. Understand that when you choose an action, you choose its consequences as well.

Mastering others is strength. Mastering yourself is true power.
— *Lao Tzu*

Character—*Character* is defined as the set of qualities that make someone or something distinctive, especially someone's qualities of mind and feeling. I wanted to start out discussing character, because your character is so important that it should define who you really are. In fact, if you do not place great value on character or if you have questionable character, there may not be very much in this book that can help you.

Your character is what makes you distinctly you. There is no cloning when it comes to your character. What do others associate you with? What do others think of when they think of you? What reputation do you have? Certain character traits are sought after in the work environment. Employers want to hire and coworkers want to be associated with those of us who are

- trustworthy,
- honest,
- hardworking,
- respectful,
- considerate,
- dependable,
- sincere,
- committed,
- loyal, and
- dedicated.

According to numerous hiring surveys, these characteristics are the most sought after in the workplace. The naked truth about these characteristics is that if you are lacking and need additional work in any of these areas, those who work with you or around you will know. As situations or incidents occur or develop, how you respond will be visible to all.

Development of character is a continuous process for all of us. If you have the desire, commitment, discipline, and determination, the areas in your character where development is needed can be improved. It's simply up to you.

Nearly all men can stand adversity, but if you want to test a man's character, give him power.
— Abraham Lincoln

Good Work Ethics—Work ethics are written and unwritten codes, principles, and values that govern decisions and actions within a company or organization. In the business world, the organization's culture sets the standards for determining the difference between good and bad decision making and behavior.

Simply, business ethics boil down to knowing the difference between right and wrong, and choosing to do what is right. When ethics are applied to business, they are used to describe the actions of individuals within a company or organization, as well as the company or organization as a whole.

Different people have different beliefs about what constitutes ethical behavior. The distinctions between moral right and wrong are not always clear. In many situations, lines between right and wrong are blurred. Such situations can lead to an ethical dilemma.

When facing an ethical dilemma, it's important to consider the outcomes of your decision-making process. One way of dealing with ethical dilemmas is to use a five-way test to evaluate your decisions. This test involves asking yourself five questions:

1. Is my decision a truthful one?
2. Is my decision fair to everyone affected?
3. Will my decision reflect positively on the company or organization?
4. Is the decision beneficial to all parties who have a vested interest in the outcome?
5. Will my decision eliminate or minimize possible litigation?

When these five questions can truthfully be answered with a yes, it is likely that the decision is an ethical one.

Another way to make decisions that are truly ethical is to use the publicity test. Ask yourself how you would feel if your actions were discovered by the media. Would you be comfortable if family or friends found out what you did? If you answer yes, chances are that your decision is an ethical one. If you do not want those who love or care about you to learn about your decision, you probably need to rethink it.

Initiative—in today's workplace, everyone is required to do more with less. The hiring process is being scrutinized and redeveloped continuously. Some entry-level job applicants are required to go through four levels of interviewing. Everyone's bottom line requires hiring high-quality people. Once they are hired, the focus is on efficiency, effectiveness, and productivity.

Managers and supervisors have so much on their plates; no one has time for baby-sitting. Once hired and trained, you've got to hit the ground running. This is where initiative comes into play. Even some government jobs, once considered safe havens by many, are no longer a place where mediocrity and complacency is acceptable. Today's job market requires you to act and make decisions without the help or advice of other people. Remember, your connections can get you the job, but only your abilities can help you keep the job.

Initiative is the ability to act and make decisions, but the inappropriate use of initiative can be detrimental to your career. As a newly hired employee, your first act after your orientation should be to become very familiar with the requirements of the job. Know what is expected of you. Second, where possible, work on getting to know your supervisor. The quicker you work on your proficiency level in these two areas, the sooner you'll be able to use initiative appropriately. As your competency level grows, so should your level of comfort with taking initiative.

When applying initiative, consider what actions your supervisor would take in a similar situation. In other words, try to envision what your supervisor will say about your actions. Think as if you are the person above your level. In other words, make decisions and develop courses of action as if your boss or supervisor were making those same decisions.

Endurance—Endurance is the capacity to bear up under difficult circumstances, not with complacency, but with fortitude that actively resists weariness and defeat.

You may wonder why endurance is so important. During an interview and upon being hired, consider your job as a marathon rather than a sprint. Obviously, marathons require endurance. Even though you may feel that you are not in it for the long haul, you must perform as if you are.

Some employees become complacent. Some also develop apathy about their jobs or what is commonly called burnout. Maintaining a high and consistent performance level is a well-sought-after workplace attribute. Employees who develop a reputation for maintaining a consistently high performance level generally are the ones assigned to demanding tasks that will enable them to earn the respect of their bosses. Working well with demanding tasks will generate well-deserved recognition that can translate into better job opportunities, more responsibility, and a higher salary.

When you get that well-deserved management or supervisor position, endurance takes on a more meaningful purpose. Leaders set the tone, and employees are always observing, monitoring, and evaluating. As a result, leaders must continually demonstrate endurance. Even when things appear bleak or you just don't feel like putting your best foot forward; you still must endure. You endure for the sake of the team, but more importantly, you endure for yourself and for those who depend on you for their well-being.

Building Credibility and Establishing a Good Reputation—It can take what appears to be a lifetime to develop your credibility and reputation. One single event, misstep, mishap, bad decision, or even the words of another person can have a lifetime negative affect on your credibility and reputation.

Complacency is a feeling of self-satisfaction, especially when coupled with an unawareness of danger, trouble, or controversy. Mediocrity is described as a state of being adequate or acceptable, but not very good; it is seen in mediocre ability, achievement, or performance. I often challenge others to identify any area of life where complacency or mediocrity is acceptable. A mindset of complacency and mediocrity in the workplace implies being average—just doing enough to get by. I constantly challenge my children, my employees, those I mentor, and myself not just to settle just for the sake of settling.

Regarding credibility and reputation, one of the most critical points in your career is when you are entering a new job, company, or organization for the very first time. It's likely that nobody knows you or anything about you. What others end up finding out about your credibility and reputation is simply up to you. When you make painstaking efforts to establish your credibility and a good reputation, your efforts will suddenly be an asset. Make no mistake about it; initially this may appear to be hard work, but it pays unbelievable dividends in the grand scheme of things. Moving forward, your credibility and a good reputation will speak for you without you having to hype or sell yourself.

Another benefit from having outstanding credibility and a good reputation is that at some point during your tenure at work, you will need somebody in your corner. There will be a point when you will very likely slip. When you do, having credibility and a good reputation is like having money in a checking account. When or if the need arises, you have something to fall back on. I know this to be true, because I have reaped such benefits during my career.

Always strive to be an excellent employee, not dishonest, not dissenting against your employer's authority—practice loyalty and protect your employer's reputation. Try to conduct yourself in an exemplary manner in every detail of your life.

Separate the Personal from the Professional–What is the difference between an amateur and a professional? A professional conforms to the standards of skill, competence, or character normally expected of a qualified and experienced person in a certain field. An amateur does something for pleasure rather than payment. For example, a professional boxer does not go around beating people up simply because he has the skills and training to do so. Boxing is what he or she is paid to do. You are a boxer when you are boxing. Boxing is what you do, not who you are. As it is with your profession, where possible, separate the personal (your nonworking life) from the profession (your work).

In non-work-related social settings, the very innocent question "So what do you do for a living?" is often used as an icebreaker. The answer to this question might reveal your salary, education level, how much power and authority you possess, and the level of respect and credibility that will be given to you during the conversation. Yes, all this information can be gleaned from that little question. There's nothing wrong with this mental chess game; you just need to be aware that it's happening. This is an example of how others who do not know you size you up.

While at home with family or while socializing among friends, your behavior and mannerism are typically casual, laid back, and unguarded. In the workplace, there is a standard, an established decorum, a professional demeanor that is expected of you. Often problems occur in the workplace when we allow that proverbial line in the sand to become blurred. Simply, it is unwise to indulge in any activity while at work that could lead to unproductive or unhealthy results. It's easy to say this, but it's difficult to refrain from engaging in such activity. People can be driven by personal agendas, and adults can often appear immature. True friendship at work is possible, but it does involve risk. Be aware of what those risks are.

I have worked with many peers and leaders who allowed themselves to be consumed by their work. Many have stated that if they had it to do all over again, they would approach work in a different way. For example, once children grow up, you can't recapture those precious moments that you missed. I advocate that the most important title in life for a man is "Daddy." When my daughters were adolescents, it didn't matter what kind of day I might have had; when I walked through the door and they ran to greet me, yelling, "Daddy's home," it made all of my frustrations disappear. Now that one of my daughters is a young adult and the other is a teen, I have to hunt them down just to let them know I *am* home.

When you are at home, make sure home matters. Ideally, establish a set amount of time to unwind, blow off steam, and get things off your chest. After doing that, let it go, refocus, and give home your undivided attention. If you share a home with someone else who works, give him or her ample opportunity to transition as well.

It is common for others to have a predetermined mindset of who you are or who you should be. While at work, what really matters is your professionalism and your ability to get the job done. When issues do surface, revert back to what really matters: your professionalism.

Sound Decision Making—If only hindsight was 20/20. If I could do it all over again. If I knew back then what I know now, my life would be different. I'm confident that a countless number of business professionals have uttered these "what if" statements. These statements are simple, yet truly profound. They relate to the decision-making processes that so many of us took for granted during our formative years.

Unfortunately, we can't turn back the clock. We can't undo the past. But what we can do from today forward is start to be wiser and smarter by focusing on making sound decisions. Today's decisions can affect us later in ways that are unimaginable. If at all possible, the key is to think about consequences before you act, rather than after you act. Perhaps every generation has pondered "what ifs," but for many of us, it is easier said than done.

Mistakes in your decision-making process are inevitable. It is the magnitude and the frequency or infrequency of your decision making that ultimately affects how you are shaped and molded. Face it; you do not know everything; none of us does. Whenever possible, make your decisions as painless as possible. When facing a difficult decision, you should

- seek advice,
- consider the consequences,
- outline the positives and the negatives,
- do research,
- pray about it (if you are a person of faith), and
- be quick to listen and slow to speak—that is, meditate on it.

Throughout life and strategically (looking at the big picture), all of us are faced with critical decisions about what I call the major crossroads of life:

- making a decision about your faith;
- making a career path decisions (and acquiring resources to pursue it), such as going to college (determining your major and/or advanced degree), acquiring a trade, going into the military, or getting a certification;
- finding a job and making a career choice;
- getting married;
- starting a family (including planning, raising, providing, educating, and role modeling for your children); and
- transitioning into the golden years (leaving a legacy, giving back; helping others, and so on).

There is some logic to the list's order. For example, you may not want to contemplate marriage and starting a family before you complete your educational goals. If this were to happen, it doesn't mean that you are a failure, but it does create challenges that you will have to overcome. Ideally, if we are able to understand the overall impact and make wise choices as they are laid out, our lives are enriched.

Avoid rashness or hastiness. Make no important decisions while agitated. Correct your faults and solve your own problems before attempting to correct the faults or problems of others

Critical Points of Emphasis:
The "Develop Self-Discipline" Operating System

1. Understand that when you choose an action, you choose its consequences as well.

2. If you have the desire, commitment, discipline, and determination, you can improve areas in your character where development is needed.

3. In many situations, lines between right and wrong are blurred. Such situations can lead to an ethical dilemma.

4. When facing an ethical dilemma, consider the outcomes of the decision. One way to deal with ethical dilemmas is by using the five-way test. This test involves asking five questions:
    1. Is my decision a truthful one?
    2. Is my decision fair to everyone affected?
    3. Will my decision reflect positively on the company or organization?
    4. Is the decision beneficial to all parties who have a vested interest in the outcome?
    5. Will my decision eliminate or minimize possible litigation?

5. When using initiative, try to think as if you are the person above you. In other words, make decisions and develop courses of action as if your boss or supervisor were making those decisions.

6. Even though you may feel that you are not in it for the long haul, you must perform as if you are.

7. Employees who develop a reputation for maintaining good performance generally are those who are assigned demanding tasks that enable them to earn the respect of their bosses.

8. One single event, misstep, mishap, bad decision, or even another person's words can have a lifetime negative impact on your credibility and reputation.

9. Complacency and mediocrity at work will make you "average." Don't just do enough to get by. I constantly challenge my children, my employees, those I mentor, and myself not just to settle for the sake of settling.

10. As you move forward, your credibility and a good reputation will speak for you without you having to hype or sell yourself.

11. There will be a point when you will very likely slip. When you do, having creditability and a good reputation is like having money in a checking account.

12. While at work, what really matters is your professionalism and your ability to get the job done.

13. Mistakes in your decision-making process are inevitable. It is the magnitude and the frequency or infrequency of your decision making that affect how you are shaped and molded.

14. Throughout life and strategically (looking at the big picture), all of us face decision making on what I call the major crossroads of life:
    - making a decision about your faith;
    - making a career path decisions (and acquiring resources to pursue it), such as going to college (determining your major and/or advanced degree), acquiring a trade, going into the military, or getting a certification;
    - finding a job and making a career choice;
    - getting married;
    - starting a family (including planning, raising, providing, educating, and role modeling for your children); and
    - transitioning into the golden years (leaving a legacy, giving back; helping others, and so on).

The "Be Trustworthy" Operating System

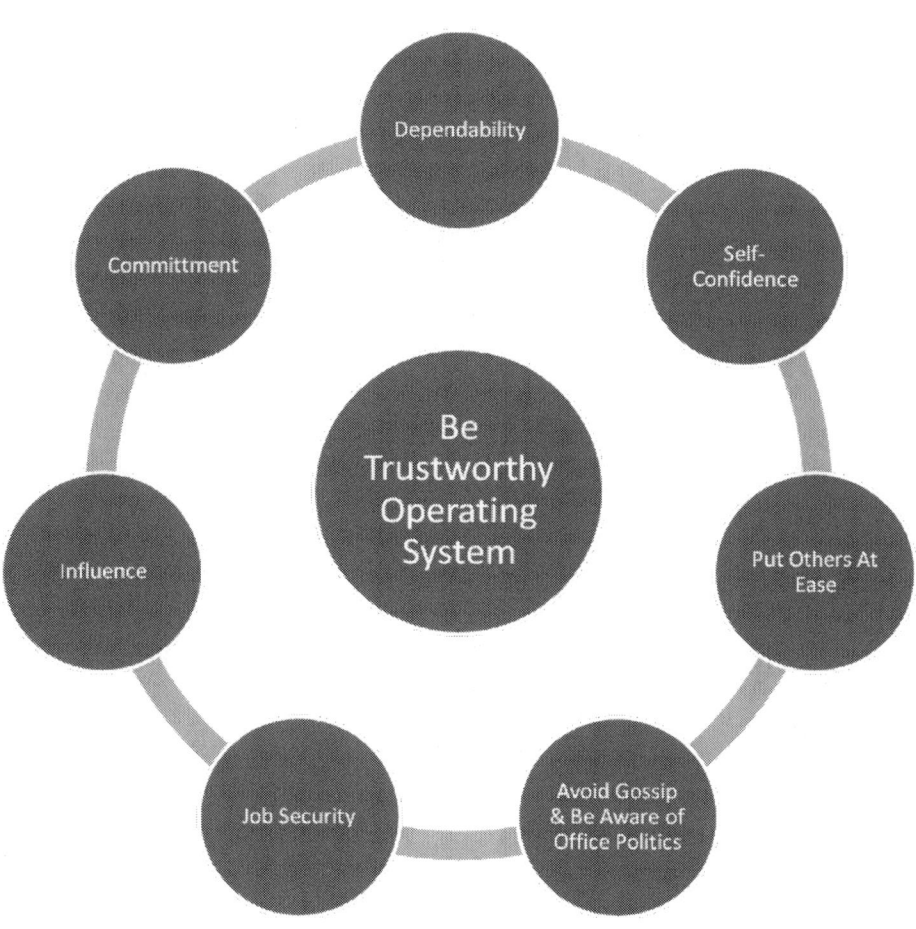

The "Be Trustworthy" Operating System

Leaders and employees are challenged more today with trustworthiness than at any point during my work life. When you consider corporate greed, corporate failures, the recession of 2008–2010, issues surrounding some prominent political leaders, ponzi schemes, the political climate, and the evening news, there appears to be credible evidence all around to support this claim. Why does such an environment exist? Does the answer lie in failed family values, failed educational system, failure to fear a higher (divine) authority, greed, or something else? What values and beliefs do you possess that impact your trustworthiness? Can you make a difference? *Will* you make a difference?

> *Take pride in being trustworthy; trustworthiness is priceless.*

Trust ranks among the most common characteristics that managers expect employees to have. Likewise, rank-and-file employees also consider trust as one of the most desired characteristics that supervisors and managers should possess. It doesn't matter which side of the aisle you represent, trust is a highly sought after characteristic in the workplace.

Trust is rebuilt by focusing not on what the other person did or did not do but on critiquing one's own behavior, improving one's trustworthiness, and focusing attention not on words and promises but on actions, attitudes, and ways of being.
— Kenneth Cloke and Joan Goldsmith

Self-Confidence—Often arrogance is confused with self-confidence. *Arrogance* is defined as overly self-assertive or self-confident, or thinking too highly of yourself. Self-confidence relates to self-assuredness in personal judgment, ability, power, and so on, as well as having no uncertainty about your own abilities or correctness. Arrogance is boisterous. Self-confidence involves quiet restraint or discipline. How do you recognize the difference between the two, particularly when you know very little about a person other than through a casual or distant observance? Self-confidence in the workplace is a positive attribute; arrogance is unflattering. Shun arrogance; embrace self-confidence.

Why is self-confidence so important? It inspires others. And it is contagious. You want to project positivity. Besides, what benefit is gained from displaying a lack of confidence? Why wouldn't you look a person in the eye while addressing him or her? Why wouldn't you shake hands firmly? Why wouldn't you want to project a positive attitude about your capabilities and potential? While on the job, you want to demonstrate confidence in your abilities.

There is an aura associated with self-confidence. *Aura* is defined as a distinctive but intangible quality that seems to surround a person or thing. Your aura projects a certain quality, impression, appearance, or persona. Sometimes you may find yourself "people watching." Do certain individuals somehow draw your interest or attention? I am not referring to a physical or sexual attraction here, but to a person's professional attire, stride, posture, uniqueness and ability to expertly handle or interact with others? These people simply have "it." They look important; they act important; you know that they are people of importance.

Your aura and self-confidence are very much a part of your personal professional presentation. My daughters told me that there is a new slang word used to describe a self-confident aura: *swag*, as in *swagger*. Well, I'll stick to *aura*; it fits my theme of professionalism just a little bit better.

Often, influential people do not have a lot of time to get to know who you really are. As a result, you may be placed in a position where you'll have to sell yourself, your product, or your services in a very short time. When this or similar situations occur, you've got to make the best of the situation. You've heard it before: a first impression is a lasting impression. You don't get a second chance to make a first impression. It is times like these when your self-confidence will make or break you.

Self-confidence has nothing to do with your title or position, but it has everything to do with knowing who you are and the way you present yourself to others with dignity.

Put Others at Ease—In many cases in the workplace, individualism is discouraged; a team work approach typically is preferred. This is not to say that in some career fields working independently is not required or expected. In any environment, putting others at ease is a welcomed skill. Make no mistake; putting others at ease may be rarely expressed publicly by your coworkers, but it is a major desired preference.

If you analyze or research the hiring process, you see that decisions are often made by hiring authorities based on their level of comfort with a potential candidate. How will you fit with the current staff? Are you a controversial figure? Are you a troublemaker? Will you be difficult to supervise? Do you have good interpersonal skills? Can you get along with others from different ethnic backgrounds? I'm not stating that I'm opposed to an employee expressing his or her individuality; I'm saying that there is a time and place for all things.

Be conscious of how your actions impact others in the workplace. If your actions or opinions are too far right or left of center (outside mainstream thinking), expect some backlash.

Sometimes certain personality issues are tolerated or even overlooked if you bring something of tangible value to the table. If you have institutional knowledge about a particular job, project, system, process, entity, or business unit that no one else has, you add uncommon value to your company. If you are a specialist or if you are really good at what you do, the higher the tolerance level will be for your individuality.

One behavior pattern in the workplace that puzzled me was how some veteran employees reacted to newcomers. It was as if the veterans wanted the newcomer to prove that he or she belonged. Or was it that everyone was simply suspicious of newcomers? Whatever the dynamics are surrounding this, it was a unique lesson in human behavior. Because I was typically the one in charge, I did everything within my power to make the new employee as comfortable as possible. For example, every new hire was required to have a meeting with me. This applied even for those in entry-level positions.

If you happen to be a new hire, the way you present yourself in the beginning could have a lasting impact on your employment with that particular company. Also, be careful who you align yourself with. Be wary of anyone who wants to give you the 411 on everyone else; evaluate others for yourself. My best advice is that you be you. Being you means being that person that won over your employer during the interview process.

Avoid Gossip and Be Aware of Workplace Politics—"Loose lips sinks ships." The last thing you want to be associated with is office gossip. Gossip can be cancerous to any business. You may think it odd that I mention the issue of gossip, but there will come a time in your career when you will be confronted with or impacted by it. Unfortunately, I was, and it drove me nuts to have to deal with such a trivial yet potentially damaging problem. I didn't anticipate having to deal with gossip from business professionals.

Prior to dealing with this issue, I had staked my management style on not chasing rumors when confronting employees about a problem or concern. But how do you approach a gossiping issue when gossip is primarily based on innuendos and hearsay? Also, gossip is so elementary, so trivial, but I was forced to deal with it. First, I sent the entire team professional development material about gossip. That didn't work. Second, I dropped subtle hints about what I was hearing. That didn't eradicate the problem. I even brought up the subject during a staff meeting. Finally, I called the employees into my office and addressed the issue with brutal honesty.

Workplace politics are like change; they are inevitable. It doesn't matter where you work or who you work for; you must be able to navigate your way in, around, or through office politics. If you mishandle workplace politics, your inability or reluctance to deal effectively with this issue can stymie or even sink your career.

Cliques are a component of workplace politics. Once in the work environment, you will simply be amazed at some of the reasons people elect not to get along with each other. You will very quickly discover that the work environment is full of people with different motives, agendas, likes, dislikes, chips on their shoulder, outright hatefulness, and immaturity. When or if you encounter or engage in such behavior, be fully prepared to deal with the repercussions. Be very careful of who you align yourself with on the job, particularly when you first arrive. Remember, if they'll do it or say it about someone else, it's just a matter of time before they'll do it to you.

There are many experienced workers who find workplace politics difficult to deal with, so workplace politics can be even more challenging for newcomers. Make no mistake about it: workplace politics can be vicious. Choose your associates carefully. Do not allow yourself to become easily influenced. If you find yourself in an unbearable situation, confide in and seek advice from a confidant, preferably one that is not connected with your job. If a situation warrants you doing so, inform your supervisor of your concerns.

If at all possible, avoid dating anyone at work, particularly a supervisor or manager. Overwhelmingly, dating at work ends in disaster. There is usually nothing good that comes out of these situations. Unfortunately, there will be those at work who prey on enthusiastic newcomers. Many companies and organizations have policies regarding fraternization and accepting gifts. It would be extremely beneficial for you to know what those polices are. There are also federal and state laws against discrimination, sexual harassment, and workplace violence, as well as laws protecting those with disabilities, such as the Americans with Disabilities Act.

I subscribe to a neutral or middle-of-the-road approach to office politics. Sometimes less is more. While at work, do not allow yourself to be sucked into the trivial, nonsense world of workplace gossip. In regard to workplace politics, I subscribe to letting the veteran politicians do the politicking. Focus on the mission, the job, and the task at hand. Be your professional best; do not worry about the rest.

Job Security—Once upon a time, job security may not have been at the top of the priority list for members of the workforce. But in the current volatile economy, job security has suddenly been thrust into the forefront and has become fashionable again. In the climate that we all operate in now, job security has definitely taken on a new meaning. During the recent recession that began in 2008, several friends and acquaintances of mine remained unemployed for an unfathomably long time. One friend with a master's degree was unemployed in excess of two years. The lives of so many were affected in ways never before imagined.

Long before the recession descended on us, I developed a very serious approach toward my employment. I never took a sick day. Really! I was rarely, if ever, late. I was outspoken when the situation required me to be, but was always tactful and respectful. I developed technical proficiency and became a subject-matter expert, which gave me a little bit more to work with than others had. I took on tough assignments and gave each and every assignment my absolute best. You get the picture. When you consistently operate at a high level, doing so under adverse conditions becomes second nature.

When downsizing, right-sizing, streamlining, or staff reduction takes place, usually substandard performers are the first to go. I've been involved in three corporate situations like this; without a doubt, working hard to be a top performer helped me to overcome these situations. In fact, while other areas within the organization were being eliminated, additional responsibility was being given to my business unit. The standards that I created for myself were much higher than those that others placed on me. During my work life, I took it personally if a supervisor had to point something out to me that I had overlooked or if I had to be told to do something more than once. I felt that a mature, professional adult should not have to have his hand held to get the job done. Also, if there was ever a threat to my work, I viewed it as a threat to the well-being of my entire family. When others depend on your ability as a provider or breadwinner, job security takes on a whole new meaning.

Both internal and external factors can impact your job security. What I'm advocating here is that, based on your performance as an employee, you have some say in your own job security.

Influence—You can wield influence without holding a position of power. Anyone can have power and authority, including someone who may not be on the upper rung of an organization's hierarchy. It doesn't matter whether we agree with coworkers who practice or wield such authority; the reality is that their authority is very real.

The "Be Trustworthy" Operating System

There are some employees I call boss interpreters. They have influence with the boss and are able to convey and interpret the boss's intentions. This lofty status has nothing to do with a job title or classification. Be mindful that sometimes boss interpreters operate subtly, while at other times they operate overtly. Their job title is not the issue. The issue is that they are real.

Boss interpreters can tell you what the boss actually means. They can tell you what the boss actually wants. They can even tell you what the boss actually does or does not like. They may or may not spend a lot of time in or near the boss's office. Boss interpreters are often executive assistants or office assistants. They control calendars, appointments, and office face time, and they are usually sworn to secrecy. If they are good at what they do, they are treasured by their bosses. Please understand however that some boss interpreters may not necessarily occupy an obvious, symmetrically-aligned operational position within the company or organization.

It is also very common for coworkers to have secret connections in the workplace. I am referring to those who may not appear influential but are connected to those with influence or power. Warning: power and authority shift from time to time as management and other personnel decisions are made. Once this happens, depending on how situations are aligned, those who wield such influence could find themselves on the wrong side of influence and power. But, typically, if you focus on being your professional best and doing the job at hand, you'll overcome or be minimally impacted by private alliances within your company.

Not only is influential power and authority real, you must find a way to deal effectively with those who possess it. A person's official status has nothing to do with his or her competence level. The "how" someone might achieve such authority varies; it's the recognition of who the boss interpreter is that's important for you.

Commitment—*Commitment* is loyalty to, a duty to, or a pledge to something or someone. It can refer to personal commitment as well as an interaction dominated by an obligation.

Earlier in my working life, I was a career military man. During my first four years of service, I took a large bonus and signed up for a job that I ended up detesting (I try not to ever use the word *hate*). I will not name the specific career field but I will share a brief description. I spent most of my time outside in the elements. This job was not linked to any civilian occupation. The work was dirty, hard, physical, dangerous and mentally taxing; there were some mechanical repairs associated with it. This career field was even closed to women.

I quickly discovered that what I had initially signed up for really wasn't me. As I progressed through that four-year commitment, seasoned veterans thought that I was good at doing the job. Some in very high places thought that I was the best they had ever seen. (I have the evidence to support this claim.) Little did they know how much I detested what I was doing. My point here is that I had made a four-year commitment. There was no sense in crying or pouting; I simply had to do the job, and I did. For four very long years, I felt as if I suffered, but I fulfilled my commitment. Afterward, I moved on to a very rewarding aviation career.

There was a positive side to all of this: I learned more about myself than at any other point in my life. I was challenged. I learned about leading men. I learned about teamwork and hard work. I was introduced to the true meaning of honor. I discovered the importance of training. I learned when to be hard and when to show compassion. I learned about toughness. And I learned about making life-and-death decisions. The most amazing thing about those four years is that everything I learned during that phase of my life benefitted me for the remainder of my military career, if not my entire life. Also, those I met during that time were some of the most dedicated and hardest working people I have ever seen. In my heart and in my mind, I had an advantage over my peers because of those four years. Commitment does pay off. Today I have no struggles with being committed to my faith, my family, and my job.

Do not make commitments too hastily; wait until you understand the full implications of any commitment you make to another. If at all possible, try not to back out of a commitment, even if it means that you have to make a sacrifice.

Dependability—Why is dependability a preferred attribute among perspective employees? Companies don't like waste; either you're doing your part to help the company or organization become profitable and productive, or you're not. Everyone must pull his or her own weight, which is what being dependable is. There is tremendous pressure on managers and supervisors. Those in positions of responsibility can't focus on their assigned duties and responsibilities if they are also required to focus on what you are doing or not doing well. When you are placed in a position to sell yourself to a potential employer or if you are trying to establish yourself in a new job, you must convince your employer that you are someone everyone can depend on. Once hired, sustaining that dependability is the real challenge. At all costs, avoid complacency.

In the current job market, your dependability will be put to test. What will you do if you are asked to stay late to work on a project when you had something else planned? When given an assignment, will you do it to your best ability? Will you complete the assignment on time? Will it be under budget? Will you have accomplished all the stated goals and objectives? Whenever your supervisor approaches you with anything, will he or she be able to depend on you? Will you grumble? Will you complain? Will you offer excuses for not meeting the deadline? Your answer to all these questions reveals to your supervisor whether or not you are dependable. Keep in mind that we are not talking about isolated situations; we are focusing on how you will handle your work consistently.

It is very satisfying for any manager or supervisor to know that he or she has an employee that is dependable when called upon.

Critical Points of Emphasis:
The "Be Trustworthy" Operating System

1. For managers, trust ranks among the most desired characteristics of employees.

2. Self-confidence is contagious. It inspires others. You want to project positivity.

3. Often decisions are made by hiring authorities based on their level of comfort with a potential candidate.

4. Be conscious of how your actions affect others in the workplace.

5. Be wary of anyone who wants to give you the 411 on everyone else; evaluate others for yourself.

6. Gossip can be cancerous to any business.

7. It doesn't matter where you work or who you work for; you must be able to navigate your way in, around, or through office politics.

8. If you mishandle workplace politics, your inability or reluctance to deal with this issue can stymie or even sink your career.

9. Be very careful of who you align yourself with on the job, particularly when you first arrive.

10. When others are dependent on your ability as a provider or breadwinner, job security takes on a whole new meaning.

11. Anyone can possess influential power and authority, including someone who may not be on the upper rung of an organization's hierarchy.

12. Not only is influential power and authority real, you must find a way to deal with those who possess it.

13. Everyone must pull his or her own weight.

14. The standards I created for myself were much higher than those placed on me by others.

The "Exercise Honesty and Integrity" Operating System

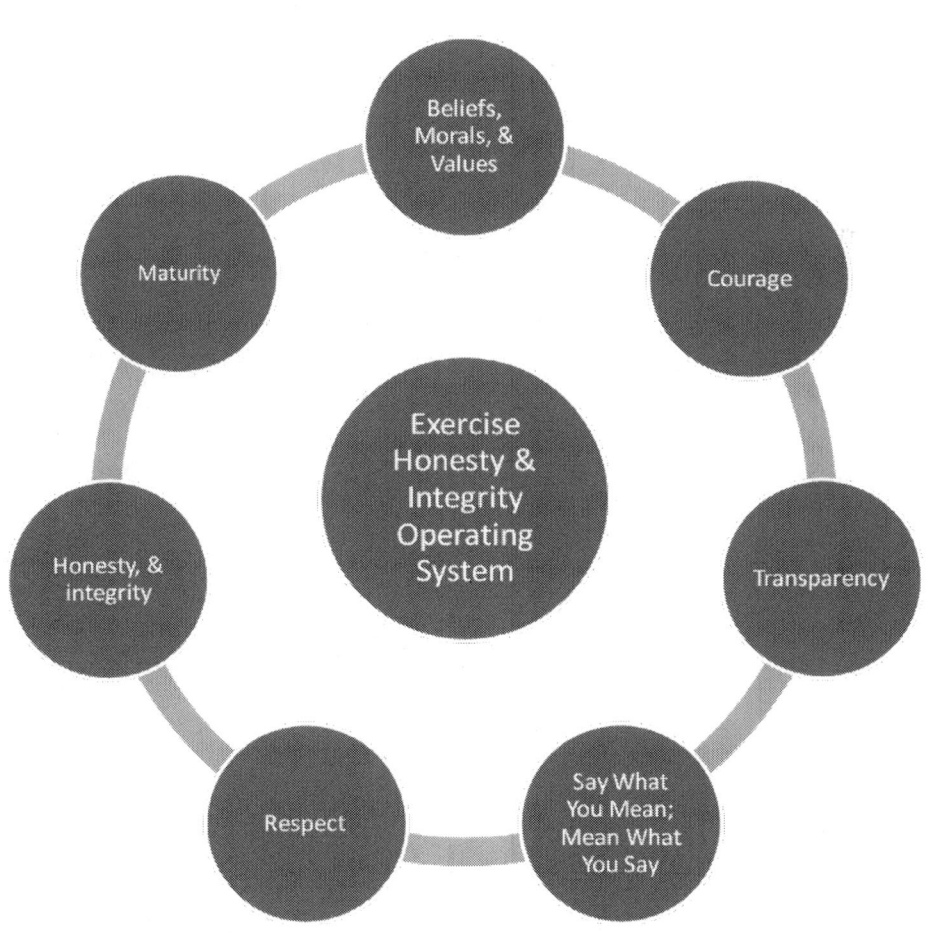

The "Exercise Honesty and Integrity" Operating System

Everyone needs a moral compass in the workplace. Many would argue that a moral compass outside the work environment is just as, if not more, important. I'm not going to argue the "where"; I am going to emphasize the sheer importance of The "Exercise Honesty and Integrity" Operating System. Your honesty and integrity reveal what direction your moral compass is pointed in. Ideally, it should be pointed in a direction that reflects positively on your faith, your family, your job, and yourself. At the end of the day, you are accountable to a higher authority as well as yourself.

> *Honesty and integrity is number one on everybody's list. The problem lies in the ability to live it day to day.*

    In looking for people to hire, you look for three qualities: integrity, intelligence, and energy. And if they don't have the first, the other two will kill you.
    — Warren Buffet

Courage—What will you do if asked to do something that violates your personal belief system? What will happen if you are asked to do something that clashes with your values or compromises your integrity? There is no right or wrong answers in these situations. The answers vary from person to person.

Others will test you just to see if you have courage. Some people make a living preying on those who appear less aggressive or weak. Some coworkers may be looking for ways to try to intimidate you in an attempt to get you to do their work. Shockingly, even some supervisors are intimidated by some employees and are afraid to assign them a task that they disagree with. When I was working my way up the ranks, my position was anyone can do anything they wanted to as long as whatever they did did not negatively impact me, my performance, or my productivity. Remember, when situations testing your courage come into play, you must seek a resolution that fits within your company's or organization's team structure and adhere to proper protocol.

Your failure to display courage when needed can create a snowball effect. Other problems are likely to surface when you fail to act decisively. Also, when you fail to display courage, your inaction will have a strange way of eating at you until you are forced to face whatever the issue is. As I reflect on moments when I lacked courage, I always promised myself that I would never allow those situations to repeat themselves.

At some point, a defining moment will surely test your courage. Actually, that defining moment may determine whether you have any courage at all. Courage is an often overlooked but admired attribute. It generally is not on display on a daily basis in the workplace. When all is said and done, the most difficult person to face is yourself.

You don't develop courage by being happy in your relationships every day. You develop it by surviving difficult times and challenging adversity.
— Epicurus

Courage is what it takes to stand up and speak; courage is also what it takes to sit down and listen.
– Winston Churchill

Transparency—Employees are much smarter today than at any time since I've been a member of the workforce. Because of this, employees are able to

The "Exercise Honesty and Integrity" Operating System

recognize genuineness among those of us who lead them. True transparency breeds trust.

Some would argue that transparency has no place in the modern-day work environment; they say it is an outdated concept. I would argue differently. I have discovered that employees accept and acknowledge people in positions over them; they just don't want you acting as if you are better than them, and they don't want to be made to feel as if you are looking down your nose at them. It is important to strike a balance between tolerance and transparency. Those in charge sometimes forget that everyone encounters a learning curve. Employees love to interact with managers and supervisors who are approachable and transparent. A person who knows that they are somebody but acts like a nobody is powerful stuff.

Find a balance between being transparent and being not so transparent. You don't want to come off with everyone as if you are a know-it-all or someone who is above reproach. There will be times when you may be assigned to a project team, for example, and it will be important for you to understand small-group dynamics. You will need to know when to speak up and when not to. It may be profitable for you to reveal some successes or even some failures, as these may be relevant to the project. How will you handle transparency issues if you find yourself in a social setting? How much should you reveal? Probing questions can be subtle or they can be brazen. How will you respond to questions about your private life? How much about your personal life should you reveal? Would your decision be different if you were with coworkers in a social setting or with a supervisor or manager in a social setting?

When using written communications, stay away from texting jargon. When verbally communicating, refrain from using whatever the latest slang may be. When socializing, it's probably not in your best interest to share too much personal information. Everyone doesn't need to know that your childhood friends called you Stick Pin or Wildman.

Some would argue that you should stay away from topics such as sex, religion, and politics. When wondering how transparent you should be, evaluate the situation, the people you are dealing with, your surroundings, the atmosphere, and so forth. After making your assessment, hopefully you'll be able to simply be yourself.

Say What You Mean; Mean What You Say—When you consistently overuse or underuse a phrase, a comment, a thought, a threat, or a promise, it loses its value.

There is great value in the spoken word. Through verbal communications, others may try to quickly determine how sharp or how slow you are. But as the old saying goes, "sometimes it's better to be seen than to be heard." Interpretation: be selective about what you say, when you say it, how you say it, who you say it to, and why you say it. Also, an old proverb that says, "Be slow to anger, be slow to speak, and be quick to listen." There is still much truth to these sayings.

The importance of being conscious of "say what you mean; mean what you say" in the workplace can never be overstated. What you say can be damaging if it is directed or received in the wrong way.

Socializing with coworkers after hours is no different from interacting with them during business hours. Even though the atmosphere may appear more relaxed, you are still being evaluated. Don't for one minute think that because it's okay for someone else to say something, it's automatically okay for you to do the same thing. The workplace hierarchy does not disappear during social gatherings. Also, do not allow yourself to become entrapped by the use of alcohol during social outings. The damage could be irreversible.

While at work, it doesn't matter if you are in a group setting, presentational setting, or individual setting, the approach should be the same. It doesn't matter what the setting may be; emphasize these things:

- Articulation is vital.
- Remain on point.
- Have command of your thoughts.
- Focus.
- Lighthearted conversation is okay when done appropriately.
- Prepare and collect yourself in advance, when possible.

Be careful how you speak and what you say to others. Please note there is a difference when you consistently overuse or underuse a phrase, a comment, a thought, a threat, or a promise for personal reasons rather than business-related re-enforcement.

Respect—Respect is a universal courtesy. Employees are required to respect a title or a position, but they are not required to respect you as a person. Respect is not relative to your position or title; just as respect is due to a CEO; it is also due to those who work in an entry-level position. I have always gone out of my way to remember the name of the employee who cleans my office. When possible, I also try to engage in small talk when this employee enters my office. Also, I've given small gifts for birthdays and during the Christmas holidays. You would be amazed at how such small acts of kindness contributed to a higher effort level being put out to ensure that all of my needs were taken care of. Surprisingly, I was amazed at the level of attentiveness to my needs when a replacement employee filled in. My guess is the regular employee told the replacement not to screw up the rapport that had been established. Respect: you must give it to receive it.

Respect in the workplace is interwoven with the quality of relationships you experience. The amount of respect or disrespect you demand or tolerate will ultimately influence the way others relate to you. If you respect others; others will respect you. Respect is not easily given; it must be earned. I believe that you reap what you sow; if you give respect to others; others will give it right back to you.

There are times, however, when it will be necessary for you to take the high road. In other words, just because someone "goes there" with you, you don't have to "go there" with him or her. Don't be made to feel as if you have to sink to the level of others when you are confronted.

Always carry yourself in a respectful manner. This is particularly true when you are the new kid on the block.

Honesty and Integrity—These two attributes reveal more about who you are and what you stand for more than any other attribute. Make it a priority to practice honesty and integrity.

Honesty is the quality, condition, or characteristic of being fair, truthful, and morally upright. Integrity is the quality of possessing and steadfastly adhering to high moral principles or professional standards. Typically, the biggest challenges associated with honesty and integrity are in situations involving right-versus-wrong issues and the possibility of having to compromise; rest assured, you will be placed in situations where you will face this. Your moral compass is priceless. How you handle these situations has more to do with you than with the situation.

If you struggle with honesty and integrity, this deficiency will permeate other areas of your life. In the workplace, you do not want to be seen as someone who has questionable honesty and integrity. That will derail your career quicker than almost anything else. If you ever allow yourself to be caught up in a situation where your boss has to question your honesty or integrity, it will be very difficult to recover. Employers place honesty and integrity at the top of their attribute wish list.

If you are able to stand on honesty and integrity, these two attributes will make everything else in your life appear less difficult. Avoid insincerity and double standards. Understand that even the slightest deviations from what you know to be right may eventually become major wrongdoings.

Maturity—Maturity starts with your ability to ensure that your personal issues are not brought into the workplace. Do not allow yourself to become consumed by trivial matters. Maneuvering your way in, through, and around your work environment requires a great deal of knowledge, savviness, and maturity.

In all likelihood, when you arrive on the scene, you will be one of the younger employees, surrounded by more tenured coworkers. I used the word *tenured* because being older doesn't necessarily equate to being more mature. Do not be surprised if you encounter older employees who are not as mature as you think they should be.

A lot of employees are territorial; you may encounter cliques; and favoritism may be prevalent. Worse yet, you could find a working atmosphere that simply may not be as professional as you think it should be. If you encounter an unprofessional working environment, your best approach is to take on the personality of a sponge; try to absorb as much as you can as quickly as you can. If at all possible, do this in a quiet, low-key manner. In situations like this, let your actions represent who you are and what you stand for.

Growth and maturity are synonymous.

Beliefs, Morals, and Values—Your beliefs, morals, and values should be your personal foundation, much like a foundation of a building. The foundation is mostly below the ground; it supports the building, transferring and distributing the weight of the building into the ground. Your personal foundation is shaped by your upbringing, education, environment, beliefs, morals, ethics, and values. Once a solid foundation is established, it will help you withstand tough times.

The "Exercise Honesty and Integrity" Operating System

Your beliefs, morals, ethics, and values define who you are and what you stand for. Whenever these attributes are on display or are called into question, others will know who you are without you having to say or do anything.

You'll know when an issue in the workplace affects your beliefs, morals, and values. At some point, a boss, peer, or subordinate will ask you to do something that you'll know is against your beliefs, morals, and values. When this occurs, you may find yourself restless, your conscience haunting you, and your internal moral fiber all twisted and knotted up. How you handle these situations is strictly up to you. Know this: you will be tested.

The work environment is diverse; that diversity is extended to many different areas. Your coworkers may not necessarily see the world or hold the same views as you do. Their approach to executing or resolving workplace-related issues could be very different. Disagreements are certain to occur. You must not only be able to maneuver in, through, and around such tenuous situations, but you also must learn to tolerate others whose beliefs, morals, and values are different from your own.

Critical Points of Emphasis:
The "Exercise Honesty and Integrity" Operating System

1. Your honesty and integrity show what direction your moral compass is pointed in. Ideally, it should be pointed in a direction that reflects positively on your faith, your family, your job, and yourself.

2. Others will test you just to see if you have courage.

3. Your failure to display courage when needed can create a snowball effect. Problems are more likely to surface when you fail to act decisively.

4. A person that knows they are "somebody" but acts like a "nobody" is powerful stuff.

5. When you consistently overuse or underuse a phrase, a comment, a thought, a threat, or a promise, it loses its value.

6. Through verbal communications, others will try to determine quickly how sharp or how slow you are.

7. Respect in the workplace is interwoven with the quality of relationships you experience. Once hired, sustaining dependability is the real challenge.

8. Just because someone "goes there" with you doesn't mean you must "go there" with him or her.

9. If you struggle with honesty and integrity, this deficiency will permeate other areas of your life.

10. Once a solid foundation is established, everything else in your life will be able to withstand tough times.

11. A defining moment will test your courage. Actually, that defining moment may determine whether you have any courage at all.

12. Socializing with coworkers after hours is no different from interacting with them during business hours.

13. Maturity starts with your ability to ensure that your personal issues are not brought into the workplace.

The "Practice Fairness and Consistency" Operating System

The "Practice Fairness and Consistency" Operating System

During my basketball officiating days, I distinctly recall how certain coaches wanted me to referee their games when they were the visiting (away from home) team versus not wanting me to officiate their games when they were playing at home. I refused to be influenced by or give in to them when they were at home but I was their friend when they considered themselves in hostile territory (away from home). My ability to remain fair and consistent, no matter the venue, was key.

> *Employees can adjust to either a laid-back or a demanding supervisor. They can't, however, adjust to unfairness and inconsistency.*

During my own trials and tribulations in the workplace, I discovered that employees are a lot like basketball coaches, next to pay, employees place fairness and consistency near the top of their priority list, particularly when issues impact them directly. Why is this so? A lack of fairness and consistency affects so many areas of the work environment, including morale, performance, attitude, productivity, and discipline. When employees show up for work, they are looking forward to doing what they are paid to do while being placed in the best possible position to succeed. A lack of fairness and consistency keeps employees from focusing on what they need to focus on: their job.

Conflict Resolution—Conflicts cause much greater damage to relationships when left unresolved. Do not respond to others out of anger; step away, and give yourself time to reflect on a proper response. *Do not allow yourself to be discouraged by small things.*

Like change, conflict is inevitable. You will endure conflict in the workplace. Face it, you are not going to get along with everyone, and everyone is not going to get along with you. And that's okay! No matter what you do, there is always going to be someone out there that does not like you and may even try to sabotage you and your career. And there are others who will forever stay focused on trivial matters.

Remember, all of us are unique. It doesn't matter how much you go out of your way to avoid conflict, it will find you. When it does, you will need to possess the necessary tools and skills to handle such situations effectively and efficiently. Your ability to handle conflict resolution properly could be the difference in you maintaining or losing your job.

When others find themselves in a testy situation with a coworker, I routinely advise them to do the following:

- Think before you act.
- Focus on the problem, not the person.
- Choose your battles carefully.
- Realize that you may not always be right.
- Admit when you are wrong.
- Become the bigger person; don't sink to the level of others.
- Stay away from the trivial.

All that really matters is that you are at your professional best while at work and that you focus on doing your job and being productive, which supports the mission, vision, and philosophy of your company or organization.

The only way to eliminate conflict is to not do anything. As long as there is movement or activity, engagement or involvement, there will always be conflict.
Dr. Samuel Chand

Minimizing Others' Complaints—We're all human, but does that give us the right to become troublemakers or whiners? There's one in every crowd; hopefully, it's not you. You know the person I'm talking about, the one that has difficulty looking in the mirror; the one that points a finger at everyone else when something doesn't go right; the one who is quick to point out a problem but is slow to offer a solution or the one who can do everyone's job better than they can. I contend that employees who fit this mode do serve a purpose. They make you a better coworker or a better supervisor. You can learn from employees who fit this description; they can help you to develop character, experience, and toughness.

I often established internal processes to help generate a desired result among my employees. In addition to aiming for a desired result, I want to challenge employees to solve their own problems at the lowest level possible first, before bringing their problems to me. Solving problems at the lowest level means going to the person you are having the problem with and attempting to bridge the gap where the problem has occurred.

If it's impossible to communicate with the person you are having a problem with, the next step is to seek a solution with the first person in your chain of command: your supervisor. If your supervisor can't find a solution, the next step would be a manager.

Whenever a problem was presented to me, I asked five basic questions to get to the core of the issue:

- Is the problem you're experiencing unethical?
- Is the problem you're experiencing immoral?
- Is the problem you're experiencing an issue of safety?
- Is the problem you're experiencing a violation of policy?
- Does the problem you're experiencing impact the mission, vision, or philosophy of the company?

Often the person who came in with the problem was amazed at his or her reaction to the questions. The answers to these questions reveal where the true problem lies and also exposes what the true problem really is.

When you identify a problem, be prepared to offer a solution. Realistically, some problems are outside the scope or capability of your chain of command, such as sexual harassment, discrimination, or workplace violence. If one of these occurs, seek outside resources, such as your company's human resources department or an employee assistance program.

Employee Performance Evaluations—Employee evaluations are a necessary component of the working environment. Once employed, one of the first items you should request is a copy of the employee performance evaluation plan. (There are other names for it, such as performance reviews, employee ratings, employee score cards, performance appraisals, and so on.) This document is important because it reveals exactly what will be expected of you while you are working in a particular position.

The employee performance evaluation process is meant to encourage ongoing, objective communications between you and your supervisor. The emphasis should be on the relationship between the company's or organization's goals and the employee's job duties, strengths and weaknesses. Employee evaluations are a positive, constructive tool to measure performance. As an employee, you should expect constant feedback from your supervisor regarding your performance.

Evaluations are typically done annually based on the fiscal or calendar year, your hire date, or a predetermined date. Periodic conferences or counseling sessions should occur at a predetermined time or as needed. When these sessions occur, both you and your supervisor should use this opportunity to address concerns that either of you have. Portions of the evaluations are subjective while other portions include tangible measurements.

The desired result of any employee performance evaluation system should be to improve each and every employee's job performance. If you and your supervisor adhere to established guidelines, the results noted on your evaluation should never be a surprise.

Seeking Personal Assistance—During your employment, it might be necessary to seek assistance for a personal problem. Depending on the type of assistance you need, your employer may or may not have the resources to handle your situation. There is internal assistance, and there is external assistance.

Internal assistance might include your supervisory chain of command, executive leadership, human resources, or safety representatives. If your problem involves someone who is within your support chain, you'll have to bypass that person and move forward and upward in an attempt to resolve your personal problem. If you fail to get what you believe is a satisfactory resolution, it is your right as an employee to continue until you find a resolution through an internal resource. However, no one can advise you on what problem you should or shouldn't go forward with; this decision is strictly up to you.

External assistance agencies are also available to offer assistance to employees. External assistance can involve a very long list of agencies and resources. One example is an employee assistance program, which varies from company to company. Assistance might be available for

- substance abuse,
- a safe working environment,
- emotional distress,
- major life events, including births, accidents, and deaths,
- financial or legal concerns,
- family or personal relationship issues,
- work relationship issues, and
- concerns about aging parents.

Other types of external assistance include the Equal Employment Opportunity Commission (EEOC), Occupational Safety and Health Act Office (OSHA), state employment commissions, state worker's compensation commissions, and state commissions on human rights. Typically, these external assistance agencies offer help for serious violations of state and federal law.

It doesn't matter whether you will ever need to get external or internal help; this information is good to know. Generally, this information should be given to you during your employee orientation. If not, your company or organization should make this and similar information available in an employee handbook.

Morale—Employee morale is often overlooked or devalued by employers. If an employer is focused, alert, and sensitive to the needs of employees and wants to have employees that are enthusiastic about work, that employer will help employees feel empowered and engaged. The acronym APPROVE can be used as a guide for employers as well as employees to bring into focus any problem that you may be experiencing.

> **Action**—Managers and supervisors are problem solvers. Any time an employee presents leadership with a problem, they have a duty and responsibility to attempt to solve whatever the problem may

be. If managers and supervisors are unable to solve a problem, it is also their responsibility to ensure that they utilize the appropriate resources to help solve the employee's problem. The same applies to ideas on improving operations; employees are encouraged to assume some ownership in their work environment. It is important to note that when they do, managers and supervisors are to ensure that proper credit is given to the person who came forward with an idea for improvement. Conversely, when an employer obviously cares enough and listens to employee input, the workers react with increased awareness and with a caring attitude toward the employer. When employees operate this way, the confidence that managers and supervisors have in their employees soars.

Personal—If my workload allowed me to do so, I made an effort each day to leave the office and walk around to all of my business unit's workstations to acknowledge as many employees as I could. It was nothing formal, just a simple hello, how are you doing? Or how is your family? No matter what kind of morning or day you may be having, make it a point to speak to every coworker you see for the first time each day. Any time an employee lost a close family member, I had my senior office assistant purchase a sympathy card for as many coworkers as possible to sign. If there was a need, and if the coworkers felt compelled to do so, they would place money in the card. Don't wait for a manager or supervisor to take actions like this. Managers, supervisors, and coworkers can also encourage decorating offices or workstations during the holidays. Be respectful of individual religious preferences. Everyone can make an effort to recognize birthdays, hiring dates, anniversaries, and special accomplishments. Make sure that all employees feel valued and appreciated for their efforts.

Praise—Employees love being acknowledged for their efforts and hard work. Praise is particularly effective when done publically. Even a simple and consistent thank-you can go a long way. I have always subscribed to the approach that if you simply take care of your business, your business will take care of you. Praise and accolades will take care of themselves. Positive written notices are also always welcomed. Saying "thank you" is the easiest way to make people feel good right away and is definitely underutilized.

Respect—Always show respect toward all coworkers. No one wants to be publicly ridiculed or belittled. To gain respect, you must first give respect. Remember, a person is not defined by the type of work he or she does. What someone does for a living does not define who he or she is as a person. Another time to show respect is when handling disciplinary matters. Discipline should always be done in private. Reasonable people understand a reasonable request, as long as it is done with respect.

Openness—Make the time to hear what each coworker is saying. This is particularly important as coworkers attempt to solve problems between themselves. There is a distinct difference between berating someone and open and honest dialogue. Always use tact and common sense so that something routine does not escalate into a major misunderstanding.

Value—Each employee should be made to feel valued as part of the team and as an individual. Remember, the level of sincerity in which your manager or supervisor values you as an employee is linked to your behavior and performance.

Enjoyment—Enjoyment in the workplace contributes to overall productivity. When employees are happy, they are more productive, have less sick time, and get along better with each other. Focus on activities that bond all employees. Remember, enthusiasm is contagious.

How Do You Handle A Difficult Boss?—We are not all made the same; thank God! We have different values, beliefs, religious preferences, personalities, backgrounds, influences, educational levels, skill sets, and even different prejudices. We are all motivated by different things. We all have different strengths and weaknesses. Because of these differences, you most certainly will have a boss that you struggle with while at work. The problem with your boss could be a lack of integrity, insecurity, promotion jettison (upward mobility), fear, inexperience, overzealousness, prejudice, envy, jealousy, unfairness, an inability to communicate, and the list could go on and on. The relevant question is how do you handle such situations?

Let me be the first to admit, *it is not easy!* Following are some recommendations that may aid you in dealing with and even resolving an issue with your boss, no matter how hard it may seem. These recommendations range from simple to severe; you must decide what the best approach is for you and your situation. Here are some options available to you to help you handle a difficult boss:

- Request a heart-to-heart meeting with your boss.
- Seek advice from a confidant; to get an impartial viewpoint, confide in someone who is unbiased or is not familiar with your boss and the situation.
- Seek advice from a mentor.
- Seek help from others within the chain of command.
- Talk to an employee assistance program or human resources representative.
- Talk to your boss's boss.
- Use a confidential complaint line (if there is one).
- Let your performance speak for you.
- Try not to stress.
- Document critical conversations.
- Remain tactful and professional.
- Think before you act.
- Try harder; be smarter.
- Take a vacation to rejuvenate your mind, body, soul, and spirit.
- Be mentally tough; try to "suck it up."
- Reassess priorities.
- Do a self-assessment and focus on becoming a better person and employee.
- Control those things that you can control.
- Seek spiritual guidance.
- Consider searching for another job.
- Retire.

As you navigate your way through and around issues with your boss, consider the warnings you would encounter when entering a construction site.

The "Practice Fairness and Consistency" Operating System

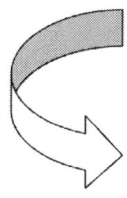  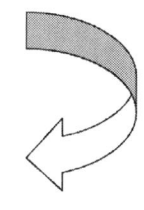

There are consequences associated with your chosen method of solving this problem. Remember, for every action, there is a reaction. Note also that one option I avoided is quitting. Simply, I do not advocate quitting. This may very well be the option your boss is attempting to force you into. If you do choose this option, secure another job before submitting your notice or resignation. Again, this situation is never easy.

The Importance of Documentation—As we catapult our way toward being a paperless society, we are being challenged to rethink our approach to documentation in the workplace. Your company may have a process for creating and maintaining files, documents, and so on. But it is essential that you understand the gravity of safe guarding, initiating, and maintaining documents that may affect you. One thing is certain: with the availability and accessibility of modern-day technology, there is no excuse for failing to properly secure documentation.

It's important to remember that your company computer is not yours. Most companies and organization have information technology staff that is capable of accessing your computer activity. I am not speaking of violating company security or confidentiality policies. The focus here is on the management of documents that are essential to your personal security, safety, trust, and credibility. During your career, there will come a time when you may be tested in this area. When the time comes, your survival may depend on how easily you are able to retrieve and produce documentation that supports your cause.

No one can predict what documents fit into what's being described here or when or even if such occurrences will take place. But I do suggest that you store personal files so that they are readily available. You need to have uncanny foresight and develop a mindset that frees you from unnecessary anxiety. My warning is this: do not depend on someone else if or when the need arises to show proof or evidence to support your case.

There is formal documentation, and there is informal documentation. Formal documentation includes your organization's guidelines involving its file system, opens records laws, official correspondence, telephone records, company cell phone usage, and so on. Informal documentation includes notes, personal records (if permitted), and so on. If you have some doubt about whether or not documents are formal or informal, check with the guidelines provided by your human resources department.

I discovered along the way that some employees are very savvy when they feel threatened by pending disciplinary actions. It is becoming increasingly difficult to get employees or coworkers to acknowledge deficiencies or shortcomings when they occur. When facing this predicament, I installed a "read and sign" process that was difficult for employees or coworkers to argue against. All mandatory training, significant policy updates, meeting notes and feedback, key handouts, and counseling sessions were documented. Whenever employees claimed that they never saw something or were never given something, their claim would be short-lived.

Setting up file folders in Microsoft Outlook or an equivalent is very important. Appropriate word association connecting your documents to your subfolder titles will save you a lot of time and grief later. Periodically go through your files and delete unnecessary clutter. Make a point to keep about thirty days' worth of "sent" correspondence.

According to the Earl Carl Institute for Legal and Social Policy, there are certain general things to remember. In your personal records, always keep a record of your work productivity; incidents on the job; significant achievements; dates, times, and a written record of statements that members of human resources have made to you; and written reprimands you have received. This makes it easier to retrieve information later on.

Always respond to written reprimands by filing a formal, typed statement disputing false claims. If there is a place for employee comments, make your protest in that section. Always be sure to sign the "acknowledge of receipt" form after receiving written warnings and reprimands, because refusal to do so could be considered insubordination. If you do not agree with the reprimand, sign your name to the acknowledgement of receipt only; above your signature write the words "signed under protest." The National Labor Relations Act gives employees rights such as this.

In certain situations, the availability or non-availability of documentation will be either a liability or an asset.

Critical Points of Emphasis:
The "Practice Fairness and Consistency" Operating System

1. A lack of fairness and consistency affects many areas of the work environment, including morale, performance, attitude, productivity, discipline, and much more.

2. Do not respond to others out of anger. Step away, and give yourself time to reflect on a proper response.

3. When others find themselves in a testy situation with a coworker, I routinely advise them to do the following:

    ← Think before you act.

    ← Focus on the problem, not the person.

    ← Choose your battles carefully.

    ← Realize that you may not always be right.

    ← Admit when you are wrong.

    ← Become the bigger person; don't sink to the level of others

    ← Stay away from the trivial.

4. An employee appraisal form is important because it reveals exactly what will be expected of you while you are working in a particular job.

5. You must remember that your company computer is not yours.

6. Always keep a record of your work productivity; incidents on the job; significant achievements; dates, times, and a written record of statements that members of human resources have made to you; and written reprimands you have received. This makes it easier to retrieve information later on.

7. Always respond to written reprimands by filing a formal, typed statement disputing false claims.

8. There are consequences associated with your chosen method of solving problems with your boss. Remember, for every action, there is a reaction.

9. When you identify a problem, be prepared to offer a solution.

10. It doesn't matter how much you go out of your way to avoid conflict; it will find you. And when it does, you will need to possess the tools and skills to handle such situations effectively and efficiently.

11. Simply, I do not advocate quitting. This may very well be the option your boss is attempting to force you into.

The "Maintain a Positive Outlook" Operating System

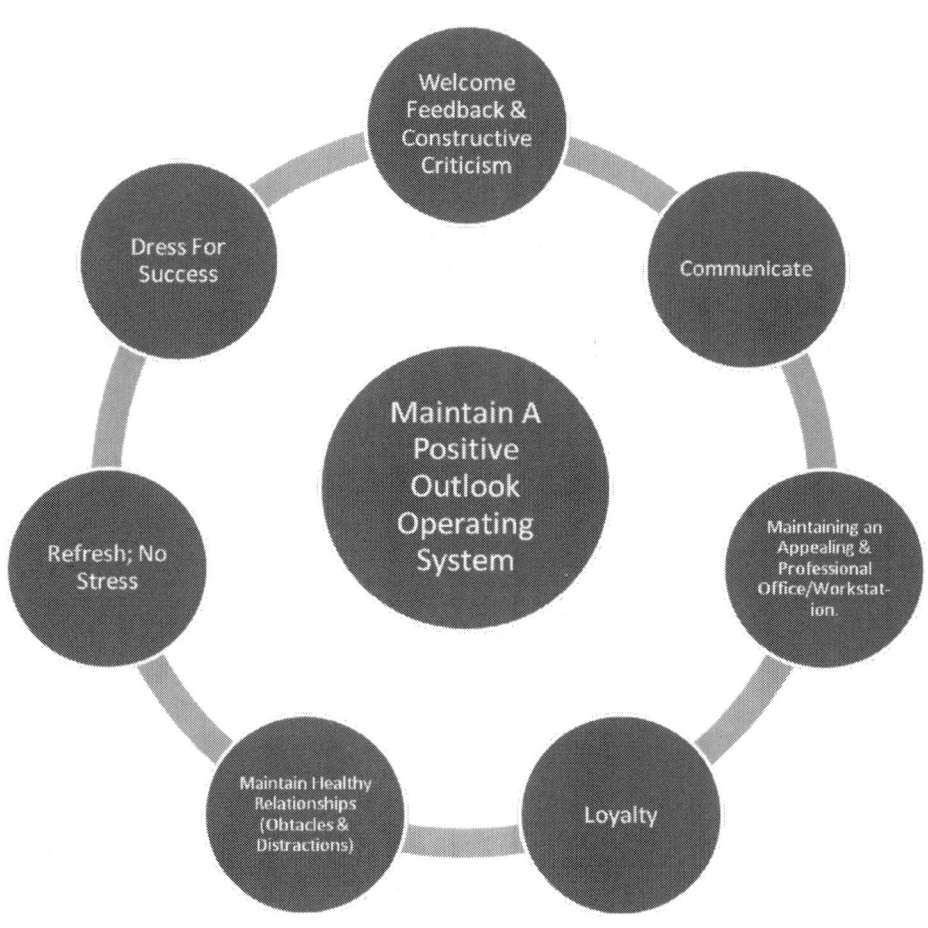

The "Maintain a Positive Outlook" Operating System

Your attitude determines your altitude. If you are a leader, maintaining a positive outlook can be infectious. If you are a member of the team, maintaining a positive outlook can earn you respect from managers and supervisors as well as from peers. You want to place yourself in a position where you have positive influence rather than negative influence. It doesn't matter whether you are in a leadership position or not; everyone has a responsibility to encourage others in the workplace.

> *Others will feed off your positivity or negativity; the choice is yours.*

   The greatest discovery of any generation is that a human being can alter his life by altering his attitude.
   — William James

Communicate—In business, you can never over-emphasize the importance of good communication. Poor communication or failure to properly communicate creates unnecessary obstacles, affects production, affects employee morale, creates waste, and even creates legal liabilities.

Communicating verbally requires a "transmitter," a "receiver," and an "acknowledgement" of what has been transmitted and received. Often the most overlooked aspect of communication is the ability to confirm or acknowledge exactly what has been communicated. A failure to do this is directly related to your ability to clearly and concisely communicate your transmission. Believe it or not, "receiving" requires you to demonstrate specific skills, including the ability to analyze and assess, patience and attentiveness. Remember, the other person or group is just as eager to share their thoughts and ideas.

The skills involved in nonverbal communication are vastly different from those in verbal communication. There are several ways people communicate, including various nonverbal forms of behavior. For example, people use gestures, facial expressions, and props. It is important to be aware of what the individual is doing as he or she is speaking. It is easy to say one thing and mean something completely different, yet it is much harder to fake nonverbal forms of communication.

A common gesture when someone agrees with what you are saying is an approving nod. In group presentations, speakers often key in on individuals to gauge whether or not their message is getting across. There are also a wide variety of hand gestures, ranging from clenching a fist in frustration to giving someone a thumbs-up in praise.

One of the primary ways in which people express themselves is through facial expressions, which is why eye contact is so crucial to communicating effectively as well as building rapport with the other person. The majority of such expressions is conveyed through the eyes and is used to reinforce what the individual wants to express.

Another very common form of nonverbal communication is the use of props to reinforce the main points. Examples of props include communicating with your hands or an object, such as a pen or pencil.

Cultural differences also can impact your ability to communicate. For example, people from a European culture may not value personal space the way Americans do. Asians may not value a firm business handshake the way Americans do. Women in positions of power may not be viewed the same way in other cultures as they are in the American culture. This is not to say that a particular culture is best or right or wrong, but that cultural differences can and will impact the way you communicate with others in the business environment.

Even though e-mail is a great tool, it has its downfalls. First and foremost, once you hit the "Send" button, in all likelihood you can't retrieve your document. If an electronic document is important, before sending it, print a copy for proofreading. Often what the eyes see and interprets on the screen is slightly different from what is seen on a hard copy. Also use spell-check. And by all means, stay away from texting jargon on all business-related correspondence.

I constantly warn my staff never to blast off an e-mail when they are angry or upset. Usually, after you have had ample opportunity to settle down, your view of the issue may change. Also, expressing "tone" during e-mail communications can be tricky. You want to come across as respectful, friendly, and approachable. You don't want to sound curt or demanding. Before sending your e-mail, verify the recipient. It's amazing how many times I've clicked the "send" button before my document was ready to be mailed.

The following should never have to be said, but it is an issue: stay away from certain websites while at work. Information technology has the authority and the capability to access anything and everything you do and say.

Over the years, I've discovered that difficulty in communicating in the workplace is the source of many problems. The primary problem with communicating is all of us have developed a different standard of what clear communication really is. We have developed criteria that inhibit us from effectively communicating with one another. For example, many of us become hoarders of information, because hoarding it gives us power. Many of us have other motives, such as dislike for a colleague; the list is potentially endless. Do not allow nonbusiness-related and unprofessional issues to prevent you from effectively and efficiently communicating with others in your workplace.

Communicating with tact is *the delicate perception of saying and doing the right thing without offending*. Tact demonstrates maturity and confidence. *Being tactful is always better than being tactless.* If you are the type of person that is very blunt with customers and co-workers, you run the risk of offending people. People do business with those they know, like, and trust. The person on the receiving end of your tactlessness may think you do not like him or her. They may think you do not want to do business with him or her because you come across as rude and offensive. Learning to use tact in the workplace means fostering better communication between you and your colleagues, as well as your supervisors, to push ahead in your career.

You don't have to be "best friends for life" with everyone, but you are required to perform your job to the best of your abilities. Doing so requires unbiased communicating. Remember, a little communication goes a long way.

Never slander anyone. Practice peace and patience with everyone, and be considerate of others. Communicate the truth exactly and accurately. Encourage others to do the same. When you communicate, make sure nothing is distorted, diluted, or deleted.

Maintain an Appealing and Professional Office or Workstation— Your office, cubicle, or workstation is a reflection of you. If these areas are cluttered, others will initially associate you with clutter. If these areas are neat and classy, others will initially associate you with neatness and class. Please do not miss the fact that I said "initially." Often an initial impression is a lasting impression. Also, an initial impression can make all the difference in the world in achieving an objective when a short-term impression is needed. However, if a short-term impression is not accurate, eventually your associates will see beyond that first impression.

Beyond first impressions, there are long-term benefits in maintaining an appealing and professional office or workstation. Aside from impressing others, your work area speaks volumes about who you are on a consistent, daily basis. A well-organized work area also helps you feel good about who you are.

You don't have to be an interior designer to understand simple workplace décor. If you struggle in this area, seek the opinion of people you trust. They will gladly tell you what is and what is not in good taste. Some of the basic décor options or considerations to consider are

- a piece of art or décor that reflects the overall theme of your company, organization, or profession,
- a live indoor plant,
- a candy dish that reflects your lighter side,

- an object, art piece, or other type of décor that elicits conversation, but nothing controversial or outside the norm,
- a family portrait,
- air freshener,
- furniture aligned to enhance the overall experience for customers, clients, coworkers, and visitors, or
- a diploma, but not too many other accolades.

Loyalty—Loyalty is not at the top of my priority list. I do think, however, that loyalty at least deserves an honorable mention in this book.

You may be a little puzzled about my comment that loyalty is not at the top of my priority list. Do not get this twisted. I did not say that I do not value loyalty. Loyalty *is* on my list, just not at the top. Loyalty has its rightful place. However, too much talk about loyalty brings up images of brown nosing and incompetence. I am fully aware that this may be a point of contention but this is simply how I feel. I have discovered that some employees (I did say some) place great emphasis on loyalty to cover up a flaw. Those flaws could include incompetence, insecurity, and timidity. On the other hand, I advocate that if you are proficient at what you do, confident, and dependable, then loyalty may not necessarily be at the top of your attribute priority list.

When I interviewed for jobs or promotions, and the interviewing process reached the point where I was asked if I had any questions of the interviewer or panel, at times I asked the question, "In this position, is more emphasis placed on competence than on loyalty?" Needless to say, that question would draw some inquisitive facial expressions. If the interviewer or panel asked why, I would downplay my response. In my mind, however, the answer to the question provided some revealing insight about the person I might be working for.

Again, loyalty is important. If you do all the things that you are supposed to do, such as show up on time, be productive, be professional, be self-motivated, and be the best employee and coworker you can be, the loyalty part will take care of itself without you having to discuss it.

Maintain Healthy Relationships; Eliminate Obstacles and Distractions—Why is it so important to eliminate obstacles and distractions? They prohibit you from performing at an optimum level.

Often, when faced with an obstacle or distraction, your focus is directed at the obstacle or distraction rather than at the business at hand.

What prohibits you from performing at your professional best? Is it a personal problem? Is it trust? Is it a relationship? Could it be your boss? A coworker? What about envy? Jealousy? Is there a communications issue? Obstacles and distractions can zap your energy, concentration, and focus. I have typically viewed unhealthy relationships, obstacles, and distractions as if they were part of an athletic competition. Once it's time to play, put on your game face and focus on meeting whatever challenges you are facing.

When looking to solve a problem, a good place to start is with you. If part of the problem is you, and often it can be, what are you doing to address that? If you think that you have no role in contributing to the obstacle or distraction, that itself is a potential problem. Once you discover the cause of the problem, you must eradicate or minimize it. The goal is to put yourself in a position where you are able to perform at your absolute best.

Often we simply tolerate obstacles and distractions for various reasons. Some of those reasons include politics, compromise, a lack of courage, inexperience, intimidation, or insecurity, just to name a few. Regardless of the reason, eliminating obstacles and distractions is necessary no matter how difficult or challenging the process may appear.

When you face someone who is adamant about arguing an opposing viewpoint, try to speak words of entreaty rather than words that are threatening. When unhappy or disappointed, refuse to respond out of anger; sleep on it if you can and give time for honest reflection. Understand that conflict causes much greater damage to relationships when left unresolved. Over the years, I've learned to accept people for who or wherever they are. It is highly unlikely that you will ever convince another adult to change who he or she is.

As a business professional, I have always felt that it is extremely important to separate your professional life from your personal life. A true professional is able to show up for work and conduct his or her business professionally without allowing personal issues to affect his or her decision making , conduct, or performance. As you focus on separating the professional from the personal, also strive to be consistent in your daily approach to your job.

The "Maintain a Positive Outlook" Operating System

If the obstacle or distraction is a coworker, focus on the problem and not the person. There is no cure-all. *Practice honesty, truth, integrity, and justice in all interpersonal dealings.*

The workplace is not a place for therapy, and your boss is not your therapist.

Refresh; No Stress—There's one thing you can count on when dealing with people; people will most certainly disappoint you. Disappointment may be generated by a family member, a friend, or a colleague. It's like change: it is inevitable. You can take all the necessary steps known to humankind in an attempt to avoid disappointment, but you cannot control the actions of others. Do not concern yourself with *if* disappointment will occur; prepare yourself spiritually, mentally, and physically so that *when* it occurs, you will be equipped to appropriately handle the situation. As the saying goes, "It's not about the situation you find yourself in; it's about you and how you handle your situation."

Work can be stressful. And some types of work can be more stressful than others. One of my favorite quotes is "The true character of a man is revealed during times of battle, rather than during the tranquility of peace." Handling yourself well during disappointments and stressful situations requires practice, patience, maturity, compromise, and self-evaluation. While at work, sometimes it is wise to take the high road. Be the bigger person.

Choose your battles wisely. I have constantly reminded my staff not to allow themselves to be drawn into unnecessary confrontational situations while at work. Typically, when you respond hastily, you regret it the next day. My advice has always been to walk away from the issue, clear your head, and readdress it after you've had an opportunity to reflect on what exactly transpired. I subscribe to the belief that leaders and professionals should always control their emotions in the workplace. When encountering face-to-face confrontations, focus on the issue and not the person; control yourself and your actions. You may be surprised how others respond in a heated situation when you flat-out refuse to emulate their unprofessional conduct or behavior. Ultimately, you lose when you lose control over your words and actions.

On a grander scale, periodic getaways do wonders for the soul. I try to take at least one major vacation each year. It has not always worked out, but I've come very close to maintaining that goal. If taking a major vacation is not possible, periodic three or four-day weekends are a great alternative. If at all possible, use some spontaneity and leave work early once in a while; your spouse or love one will applaud your efforts.

Dress for Success—Should you wear business attire? Do you go with business casual? Are there casual Fridays? Are uniforms required? Are jeans acceptable?

As quickly as possible, find out what the corporate culture is in your company or organization. Corporate culture is the beliefs and behaviors that determine how employees and management interact and handle business transactions. Often corporate culture is implied, not expressly defined, and develops organically over time from the cumulative traits of the people the company hires. A company's culture will be reflected in its dress code, business hours, office setup, employee benefits, turnover, hiring decisions, and treatment of clients, client satisfaction, and every other aspect of operation. Once you determine what the corporate culture or established dress code policy is, you will be able to make an informed decision about your attire. Ideally, you'll know about the work attire before your first day on the job.

Whatever the accepted attire may be, the common denominator is to be neat, well groomed, and clean. Many may think this goes without saying, but I have discovered that you can't take anything for granted. Standard grooming practices are not as obvious as you may think. To my disappointment, I have had to address hygiene issues with employees who were well beyond the age of knowing better.

Body piercings and tattoos have become more acceptable than they were in the past. How well they are accepted depends again on the corporate culture or established dress code policy of your company or organization. In all likelihood, body piercings and tattoos may be more of a hindrance than an encouragement. When in doubt, dress conservatively. Another approach is to observe how your supervisor dresses and to try to emulate his or her attire.

Generally, these are looks females should avoid in the workplace:

- too sexy (see-through lace, miniskirts, spaghetti straps, sheer sundresses, strappy stiletto sandals, cleavage showing)
- too casual (jeans, shorts, T-shirts, hats, sneakers)
- sloppiness (wrinkled clothing, too many layers, baggy clothes)

- stilettos
- distracting Jewelry
- flip-flops

Generally, these are looks males should avoid in the workplace:

- un-tucked shirts
- sagging pants
- sandals
- shorts
- hats or caps indoors
- sunglasses indoors
- jewelry, unless it is understated

Your attire and appearance should be an asset, not a liability. Try to avoid bringing unnecessary attention to yourself.

Welcome Feedback and Constructive Criticism—If you have the desire to improve so you can be the absolute best you can be, you must develop the ability to accept feedback and constructive criticism from others.

There is a distinct difference between constructive and non-constructive criticism. Constructive criticism is intended to build you up and help you to overcome your shortcomings. Criticism is destructive, can be painful, and does not help you improve. To be effective, you must be willing to accept feedback and constructive criticism from reputable people. Let me assure you, there will be plenty of feedback and criticism from coworkers. Be aware of coworkers who are divisive. It's also important to understand that agreement is not always positive and disagreement is not always negative; people can disagree with you and still add value.

Feedback and constructive criticism come in very different forms. These forms include counseling, coaching sessions, mentoring, and impromptu, informal exchanges. The ability to accept feedback and constructive criticism reveals so much about you. Sometimes it isn't easy to listen to someone tell you how you can and should work toward improving yourself. However, this is a necessary component of the workplace culture.

Your level of maturity, willingness to improve, self-control, and attitude are on full display when receiving feedback and constructive criticism. Try not to become too defensive in these situations. You'll have to decide what to file and what to discard. Don't be naïve about this; whenever your supervisor engages you with feedback and constructive criticism make no mistake about this: he or she is keeping tabs and will remember.

Depending on the type of industry you work in, you might receive feedback and constructive criticism from clients or customers. Remember, they have a right to voice their opinions or concerns. When this occurs, remain calm and professional when presenting your side of the story. For whatever it's worth, use these situations as a learning experience or teaching moment.

It is often said that the most difficult person to evaluate is yourself. While in positions of authority, I have spent an inordinate amount of time doing self-evaluations with the full intention of continuing to enhance my personal and professional development.

True leaders are always listening and learning. You can learn from others daily.

Critical Points of Emphasis:
The "Maintain a Positive Outlook" Operating system

1. As a member of a team, maintaining a positive outlook can earn you respect from managers, supervisors, and peers.

2. A failure to communicate properly will create unnecessary obstacles, affect production, affect employee morale, create waste, and even create legal liabilities.

3. An initial impression can make all the difference in the world in achieving an objective where a short-term impression is needed.

4. Often, when faced with an obstacle or distraction, your focus is directed at the obstacles or distraction rather than the business at hand.

5. When looking for a resolution, a good place to start is with you.

6. Once you determine what the corporate culture is, you will be able to make an informed decision about your work attire.

7. Handling yourself well during disappointments and stressful situations requires practice, patience, maturity, compromise, and self-evaluation.

8. Your level of maturity, willingness to improve, self-control, and attitude are on full display when receiving feedback and constructive criticism.

9. It is often said that the most difficult person to evaluate is yourself.

10. Obstacles and obstructions prohibit you from performing at an optimum level.

11. The workplace is not a place for therapy, and your boss is not your therapist.

12. Leaders and professionals should always control their emotions in the workplace.

13. Whatever the accepted attire may be, the common denominator is to be neat, well groomed, and clean.

14. Do not allow nonbusiness-related and unprofessional issues to prevent you from effectively and efficiently communicating with others in the workplace.

15. As a business professional, I have always felt that it is extremely important to separate your professional life from your personal life.

16. To be effective, you must be willing to accept feedback and constructive criticism from reputable people.

The "Personal and Professional Development" Operating System

The "Personal and Professional Development" Operating System

There's only one corner of the universe you can be certain of improving, and that's your own self.
— Aldous Huxley

Your personal and professional development is solely your responsibility.

Personal and professional development is a continuous, ongoing process. You must assume accountability and responsibility for your career or lack of a career. No one owes you anything. To many, this is a harsh reality. Millions of jobless are looking for a job. And millions who already have a job are surely looking for a promotion, more money, status, and power. What separates you from everyone else? The answer starts with your uniqueness. There is no one else out there like you. So, what do you bring to the table?

Formal Education—For the current generation and generations to come, a lack of education is simply no longer an option. The seed of education should be planted by parents in the home at an early age. For many, college preparation begins at middle school or junior high level. Why is this so important?

Question: What is the average income for high school and college graduates?

Response: In 2010, some 62 percent of young adults ages 25-34 in the labor force were employed full time throughout a full year. The percentage of young adults working full-time, full-year was generally higher for those with higher levels of educational attainment. For example, 71 percent of young adults with a bachelor's degree or higher were full-time, full-year workers in 2010, compared with 57 percent of young adults with a high school diploma or its equivalent. Among young adults employed full-time, full-year, higher educational attainment was associated with higher median earnings. This pattern of higher earnings corresponding with higher levels of educational attainment was consistent for each year shown between 1995 and 2010. For example, young adults with a bachelor's degree consistently had higher median earnings than those with less education. This pattern held for male, female, White, Black, Hispanic, and Asian subgroups.

In 2010, the median of the earnings of young adults with a bachelor's degree was $45,000, while the median was $37,000 for those with an associate's degree, $29,900 for those with a high school diploma or its equivalent, and $21,000 for those who did not earn a high school diploma or its equivalent. In other words, in 2010, young adults with a bachelor's degree earned 22 percent more than young adults with an associate's degree, 51 percent more than young adult high school completers, and 114 percent more than young adults who did not earn a high school diploma. In 2010, the median of the earnings of young adults with a master's degree or higher was $54,700 or 22 percent more than young adults with a bachelor's degree. (U.S. Department of Education, National Center for Education Statistics. 2010. *The Condition of Education 2010* (NCES 2010–028), Indicator 17.)

Median annual earnings of full-time, full-year wage and salary workers ages 25-34, by educational attainment: 1995-2010

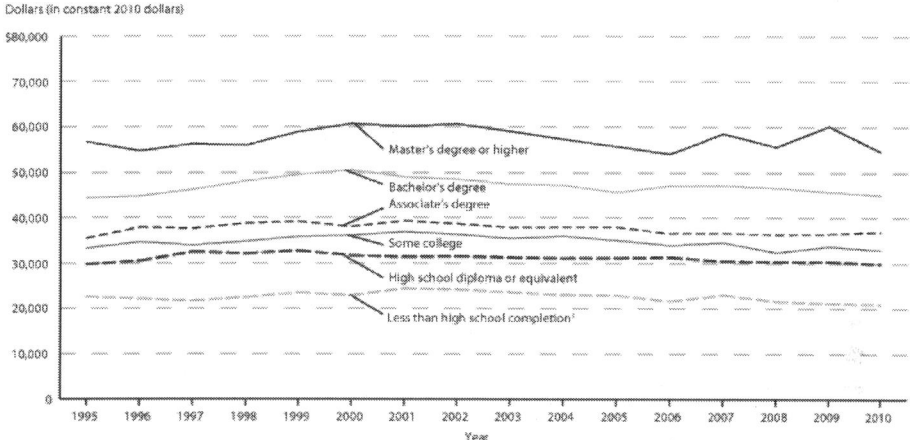

[1] Young adults in this category did not earn a high school diploma or receive alternative credentials such as a General Educational Development (GED) certificate. NOTE: Earnings are presented in constant dollars by means of the Consumer Price Index (CPI) to eliminate inflationary factors and to allow for direct comparison across years. *Full-year workers* refers to those who were employed 50 or more weeks during the previous year; *full-time* workers refers to those who were usually employed 35 or more hours per week. Race categories exclude persons of Hispanic ethnicity.

(U.S. Department of Commerce, Census Bureau, Current Population Survey (CPS), Annual Social and Economic Supplement, 1996–2011.)

(Aspiring Professionals) How to Enhance Your Professional Performance and Productivity

Median annual earnings of full-time, full-year wage and salary workers ages 25-34, by educational attainment and sex: 2010

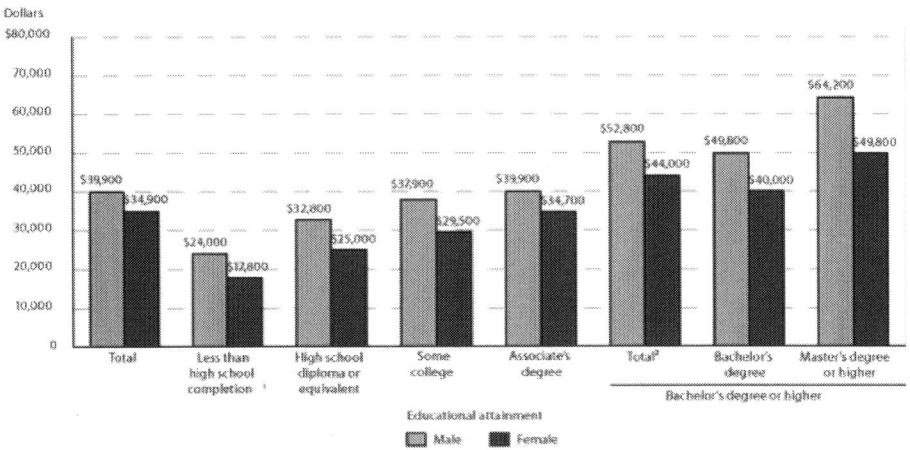

[1] Young adults in this category did not earn a high school diploma or receive alternative credentials, such as a General Educational Development (GED) certificate.

[2] Total represents median annual earnings of young adults with a bachelor's degree or higher. NOTE: *Full-year workers* refers to those who were employed 50 or more weeks during the previous year; *full-time* workers refers to those who were usually employed 35 or more hours per week.

(U.S. Department of Commerce, Census Bureau, Current Population Survey (CPS), Annual Social and Economic Supplement, 2011.)

Postsecondary Education
Economic Outcomes

Median annual earnings and percentage of full-time, full-year wage and salary workers ages 25–34, by educational attainment, sex, and race/ethnicity: Selected years, 1995–2010

Educational attainment, sex, and race/ethnicity	Median earnings [In constant 2010 dollars]									Percentage of labor force participants who worked full-time for a full year in 2010[1]
	1995	2000	2005	2006	2007	2008	2009	2010		
Total	**$35,800**	**$38,000**	**$36,800**	**$37,000**	**$36,800**	**$36,500**	**$38,600**	**$37,400**		**61.9**
Less than high school completion[2]	22,700	22,900	22,900	21,600	23,100	21,600	21,200	21,000		44.9
High school diploma or equivalent	29,700	31,700	31,100	31,300	30,500	30,400	30,400	29,900		57.0
Some college	33,300	36,500	35,000	34,000	34,600	32,400	33,700	32,900		58.1
Associate's degree	35,500	38,000	37,900	36,600	36,600	36,400	36,500	37,000		63.6
Bachelor's degree or higher	47,200	50,600	49,000	48,500	50,300	50,600	50,700	48,700		71.4
Bachelor's degree	44,300	50,500	45,600	47,000	47,100	46,600	45,700	45,000		71.2
Master's degree or higher	56,700	60,700	55,800	54,100	58,500	55,600	60,200	54,700		71.7
Male	38,500	40,500	39,100	37,900	39,900	40,500	40,700	39,900		64.5
Less than high school completion[2]	25,400	25,200	24,500	23,700	24,200	24,300	23,000	24,000		47.4
High school diploma or equivalent	34,300	36,500	33,400	32,400	32,400	32,400	33,400	32,800		60.6
Some college	37,100	40,300	39,000	37,600	38,600	36,700	39,300	37,900		62.0
Associate's degree	36,900	44,300	43,400	40,700	41,800	40,800	42,400	39,900		68.6
Bachelor's degree or higher	53,200	58,100	55,800	53,700	54,200	55,600	55,300	52,800		75.0
Bachelor's degree	50,000	56,700	50,200	53,300	52,500	53,600	51,300	49,800		75.4

85

(Aspiring Professionals) How to Enhance Your Professional Performance and Productivity

Educational attainment, sex, and race/ethnicity	Median earnings [In constant 2010 dollars]									Percentage of labor force participants who worked full-time for a full year in 2010[1]
	1995	2000	2005	2006	2007	2008	2009	2010		
Master's degree or higher	63,300	69,500	61,400	62,600	64,900	65,100	70,400	64,200		74.0
Female	31,200	35,100	33,500	33,500	34,600	34,400	35,500	34,900		58.7
Less than high school completion[2]	18,500	19,000	18,800	19,300	18,700	16,700	19,300	17,800		39.4
High school diploma or equivalent	25,200	27,700	26,700	25,500	25,300	25,200	25,400	25,000		51.1
Some college	28,600	31,600	31,200	30,200	31,500	29,300	29,700	29,500		53.6
Associate's degree	34,300	33,700	32,700	32,400	32,600	32,900	31,400	34,700		59.1
Bachelor's degree or higher	42,600	45,600	44,400	44,300	45,100	45,500	45,700	44,000		68.0
Bachelor's degree	39,900	44,200	41,900	43,100	41,900	42,200	40,800	40,000		67.2
Master's degree or higher	49,400	52,600	52,400	51,800	52,800	51,400	54,900	49,800		70.0
White	37,200	41,400	39,100	40,000	42,000	40,500	40,700	40,000		63.3
Less than high school completion[2]	25,100	26,300	25,600	27,000	25,200	25,900	25,100	25,000		39.5
High school diploma or equivalent	31,400	35,000	33,400	32,400	31,500	31,600	32,500	32,000		57.1
Some college	34,300	37,900	35,600	35,900	36,700	33,400	35,600	34,800		57.0
Associate's degree	37,100	40,100	38,700	37,400	38,700	39,500	40,500	39,700		63.9
Bachelor's degree or higher	48,600	50,600	49,800	48,500	50,400	50,600	50,700	49,500		71.7
Bachelor's degree	45,800	50,600	45,800	47,900	47,200	47,500	45,700	45,900		71.5
Master's degree or higher	56,900	60,600	55,800	53,900	57,500	55,500	58,500	54,300		72.3
Black	30,000	31,700	31,900	32,400	31,500	30,400	30,500	31,600		57.7
Less than high school completion[2]	19,800	21,000	22,800	19,300	19,800	18,300	22,600	20,300		30.5
High school diploma or equivalent	25,700	27,700	25,600	27,000	27,200	26,300	25,400	25,000		53.6
Some college	31,400	32,800	32,400	30,000	31,400	30,000	29,500	29,300		56.2
Associate's degree	31,400	31,500	31,100	31,200	31,000	31,100	28,200	31,400		61.5
Bachelor's degree or higher	39,200	43,800	43,300	42,800	41,800	44,900	45,300	41,000		72.4
Bachelor's degree	37,200	41,500	39,400	39,800	41,000	40,500	40,700	39,500		71.1
Master's degree or higher	47,400	51,100	48,100	51,200	47,300	53,100	54,000	49,100		76.5

The "Personal and Professional Development" Operating System

Employee Training Programs—After being hired as a supervisor during a point in my career, I asked my manager about training. I asked a few very simple questions like, who is going to train me? Where is the training manual? How long will my training last? When I discovered that none of my questions could be answered, I was astonished. How could it be? How could a business not have a formal employee training program in place? As time passed, I made it my mission to ensure that everyone who came after me had a formal training program so they wouldn't have to endure what I had endured.

Whenever I transitioned into a new position, after being introduced to my new supervisor and being told what was expected of me, my very next goal was to work as hard as I could to bring myself up to speed with the competencies of the job. I later realized that even if everything was laid out for me, the ultimate responsibility for meeting the competencies of the job rested with me. Some organizations have manuals; others have a formal program to assist you. Still others may assign someone to oversee your transition until you are up to speed. Or maybe, you're just plain fortunate if a fellow coworker happens to take a liking to you and doesn't mind helping you. Whatever the method may be, you must take advantage of all available resources to bring yourself up to speed as quickly as possible.

The initial on-the-job period is crucial to your future. You've heard it before: "A first impression is a lasting impression." Your employer is wondering if he or she made a wise choice by hiring you. You may be wondering if you made a wise choice by accepting the position. Not only are you and your new employer essentially wondering the same thing, coworkers are also evaluating you, feeling you out. Do not succumb to the pressure; just be yourself.

"The only thing worse than training employees and losing them is not training them and keeping them."
— Dr. Samuel Chand

Know Your Company's Policies and Procedures—Every business, organization, or company has its own unique way of doing business. Along with a mission, vision, and philosophy, there are policies and procedures. It doesn't matter if the policies and procedures are related to human resources, operations, maintenance, logistics, planning, or safety, the sooner you are familiar with what they are, the better. You can't play the game effectively if you don't know the rules. You'll never know when policies and procedures may become your lifeline. They are designed to protect you, your company, and the clients and customers you serve. But remember, your protection becomes less effective the more you stray, the more risks you take, and the more inconsistent you become in the use, knowledge, and application of policies and procedures. Do not rely on anyone else to have your back.

A key component to applying and knowing applicable policies and procedures is your ability, your desire, and your discipline to adhere to whatever they state. I have discovered that simply knowing the policies and procedures is not the downfall of most employees; their primary downfall is the inability to execute the policies and procedures they are familiar with. Their secondary downfall is (unbelievably) that they simply don't like to read. I'll admit that sometimes reading that stuff can be downright boring, but this is no excuse. Your security and overall success may depend on how knowledgeable you are in this area. Don't be ill prepared because of apathy or lack of motivation.

Procedures are written guidelines that help guide day-to-day operational functions and decision making. Each company or organization will typically establish its own operational procedures. Once you are familiar with and understand the guiding principles of written guidelines, this will help you carry out your day-to-day duties and responsibilities. Each functional area is likely to have its own established procedures. Procedures delve into the "how" of things. Examples of procedures include a company's written guidelines on human resources complaints, sexual harassment, or vacations procedures.

Observe Others—Where's a good place to "people watch"? I would suggest the workplace is one of the most common places to "people watch'. Think about it: at work, people watch people. Employees watch to see how one employee is treated over another. They watch to see who, if anyone is getting preferential treatment. Coworkers watch to see what you're wearing. They watch to see who's hanging out with whom during lunch or nonbusiness hours. They watch and listen to try to determine who's in what clique. And of course, everyone watches the boss. Are you inclined to agree that some of the most consistent yet subtle people watching occur in the workplace?

The "Personal and Professional Development" Operating System

I want to challenge you to people watch at work for a totally different, more beneficial reason. In the workplace, you will encounter people that you admire and you will encounter people you simply do not admire. Ironically, you can learn from the persons you don't admire just as much as you can learn from the person you do admire. For some strange reason, I kept mental notes on managers and supervisors that I have had over the years. I observed them closely and picked up and stored habits, styles, mannerisms, techniques, best practices, and worst practices.

Take what you think are the good qualities, and learn from what you think are the bad qualities. Mesh the two to fit your personality, your disposition, your values, and your beliefs. As a result, you will create your own aura, leadership style, and professional ethics. This is similar to when you were growing up; your upbringing affected you immensely. The positive and not-so-positive observations and relationships that you encounter can have a major impact on you as you navigate your way through the demands of the workplace and your career.

Observing others in the workplace is a subtle yet effective way to work on self-improvement.

Find and Become a Mentor—Mentoring is a relational process in which a mentor, who knows or has experienced something, transfers that something (wisdom, information, experience, confidence, insight, relationship, or status) to a mentee at an appropriate time and manner, so that it facilitates development and empowerment.

Often when I am mentoring others, I thank them for allowing me to mentor them. Little do they know their mentor learns just as much about himself as the mentee learns about themselves. This technique is called "reverse mentoring." Sometimes, when mentoring others, I have no idea where the conversation is going; better yet, I have no idea what my responses will be.

I have come to realize that the most important aspect of mentoring is listening. When you listen, you are able to share your experiences that apply to the situation. In mentoring situations, I have allowed myself to be led by my inner spirit. More importantly, rarely do I give advice. What I do is explore options and possibilities when I am speaking. Once the options and possibilities are thoroughly explored, I leave it up to the mentee to select what is best for him or her.

How do you choose a mentor? What are the criteria for selecting a mentor? In choosing, there is no right way or wrong way. Depending on you and who you're going to ask, the approach can be subtle or bold. Over time, I've just focused on developing a relationship with a person, and eventually the relationship developed into a mentoring relationship. Here are some of the qualities that you should look for in a mentor:

- maturity
- experience
- accomplishment
- earned respect
- integrity
- good reputation
- availability
- an example to others

This is not an all-inclusive list; it is an essential start that can be modified.

Just because you ask someone to mentor you, doesn't mean that he or she is obligated to say yes. When I am asked to mentor someone, I evaluate the potential of the person asking, just as he or she evaluates me. I have to see something in that person. I have to determine if the endeavor is a worthy one. I've never agreed to mentor someone I didn't know.

Each of us has battles to fight and needs wise and frequent advice to fight them well.

Timeliness and Staff Meetings—In business, not being on time is unacceptable. Deals are lost because of lateness. Money is lost because of lateness. Production is negatively impacted because of lateness. Worse case, people are terminated because of lateness.

Failure to be on time reflects negatively on you. It also reflects negatively on those you represent. Being late sends the message that you are potentially disorganized, undisciplined, unmotivated, inconsiderate, disrespectful, or unprofessional. I don't think any one of us wants to be associated with this type of stereotypes. Ideally, make it a habit to show up ten to fifteen minutes early. If you don't want to actually enter a meeting or appointment too early, it's okay to linger in the lobby or parking lot, or simply to use the time reviewing notes. Not to worry, someone else who thinks like you will be early to.

The "Personal and Professional Development" Operating System

Basically, there are three types of meetings:

- announce and inform
- obtain the support of participants
- focus on problem solving

Elements of a good meeting include

- preparation
- agenda
- leader or facilitator control
- purpose
- group participation
- location
- provide tools for effective communications
- make time for open discussion and interaction
- summarization
- review of action items

I have attended meetings, presentations, and training sessions where the person responsible for facilitating is still setting up as participants arrive. I have never understood this approach or mindset. Not only is it unprofessional to conduct yourself in this manner, but it is also reflects negatively on you and the company or organization you represent. When you are assigned the task of being the person in charge of a meeting, presentation, or training session, try an "advanced function check." This check is simply what it says it is: check out the operability of your equipment, facilities, and material well in advance of the participants' arrival. If you have ever been in a situation where things were out of order prior to a scheduled training session or presentation, and if you are honest, this ill-preparedness impacted the quality of work you participated in or were responsible for.

At all cost, avoid airing dirty laundry in meetings. The meetings before the meeting are where the real decisions are made. Your manager or supervisor should never be surprised by anything you say in a meeting format. If you continuously keep your manager or supervisor updated, your comments during meetings should be limited to recaps unless the line of questions is related to a new initiative. If you know before the meeting what the primary topic of discussion will be, take advantage of the opportunity to research the topic of discussion and prepare notes and talking points. Preparation is the key to achieving positive meeting results.

Motivation, Focus, and Ambition

Place emphasis on what you can control. Do not waste time, energy, and effort on what you can't.

Everybody loves a winner. Everybody wants to be associated with success. This is why people flock to whatever the latest, greatest trend may be. Being a winner and being associated with success does wonders for the individual psyche. Becoming a winner, becoming a success, is not easy. In most cases, becoming a winner and being successful requires very hard work involving motivation, focus, and ambition (plus commitment, dedication, and resources).

Motivation—As I think back on my introduction to military basic training, I do so with amusement. I'll have to admit that at the time of my initial encounter with a burley drill sergeant, the situation was not all that amusing. Imagine, if you can a young, scrawny, independent, know-it-all eighteen-year-old with long, seventies hair, trying to follow instructions by lining up in something called a formation and being confronted by what appeared to be an angry, venom-spewing, uniform-clad Vietnam veteran. Imagine the yelling, intimidation, fear, bewilderment, and undercover snickering all rolled into one set of wild emotions. Later I began to understand that the transformation had begun. The drill sergeant's job was to instill discipline and motivation, and transform my comrades and me into becoming soldiers.

While your introduction to motivation may not be this dramatic, the transformation from an eager college grad into a business professional is just as important. What motivates you? Money? Power? Fear? Status? Success? Failure? Responsibilities? Faith? Security? Love? Parents? Whatever the answer is, does your level of motivation depend on someone else? Ideally, you should be able to motivate yourself—ideal, but not always true. Over the years, I became upset with myself if a supervisor had to point something out that I missed or overlooked. My level of motivation is based on internal drive rather than external prodding. This type of approach will help see you through a long and gratifying career.

The "Personal and Professional Development" Operating System

An unmotivated or disgruntled employee is not only unproductive, but also irritating.

Long shots do come in and hard work, dedication, and perseverance will overcome almost any prejudice and open almost any door.
— John H. Johnson

Focus—*Do not become discouraged; you must pass through the clouds before you reach the stars.*

Typically, promotions, upward mobility, promotion jettison—or whatever the current catchphrase is for getting ahead—revolves around timing, your education and training, and who you know.

Typically, when striving for a position or promotion, there's not a lot that separates one candidate from another on paper; everyone has an impressive resume. It's usually the little things that make the difference—the intangibles. *Do not spurn small advances. The process toward being the best you can be is made up mostly of small steps, rather than major ones.* Your motivation, focus, and ambition could be what separate you from the rest of the pack.

Think of focus as your personal GPS system. You'll always know exactly where you are going when you focus. Seldom will you stray; your focus allows you to stay on the path toward achieving your goal.

Personal strength is not measured in good times but in bad.

Ambition—*Don't simply follow the trail; become a trailblazer.*

When I was describing the significance of the ten chapters, I stated, "We should strive to be the best we can be and to reach the highest levels we can reach." This mindset, belief, and approach are intimately linked to your ambition. Ambition is the desire for personal achievement. It provides the motivation and determination necessary to help give direction to life. Ambitious people seek to be the best at their pursuits.

While mentoring others, I have discovered that generally there are two ways to evaluate the ambition level of upstarts (young, aspiring professionals): (1) those that talk about their motivation, focus, and drive and (2) those that execute their plans based on their motivation, focus, and ambition.

When I was involved in sports officiating, I had the privilege of working around a few world-class athletes. They had and used their God-given talents to help achieve their goals. I became enthralled with the fact that they had something in common: they all had tremendous focus, dedication, ambition, and work ethics.

It is no secret that many of us covet success, prestige, respect, and status. The problem is that many of us are not willing to do whatever it takes to achieve the things that we covet.

Chase your passion, not your pension.
— Denis Waitley

Critical Points of Emphasis:

The "Personal and Professional Development" Operating System

1. You must assume accountability and responsibility for your career or lack of a career.

2. Even if everything was laid out for me, the ultimate responsibility for meeting the competencies of the job rested with me.

3. Job-related policies and procedures are designed to protect you, your company, and the clients you serve.

4. Ironically, you can learn from the persons you don't admire just as much as you can learn from the person you do admire.

5. I have come to realize that the most important aspect of mentoring is listening.

6. Some of the qualities that you should look for in a mentor include

    ← maturity

    ← experience

    ← accomplishment

    ← earned respect

    ← integrity

    ← reputation

    ← availability

    ← an example to others

7. Deals may be lost because of lateness.

8. Place emphasis on what you can control. Do not waste time, energy, and effort on those things you can't.

9. My level of motivation is based on an internal drive rather than external prodding.

10. Your motivation, focus, and ambition could be what separate you from the rest of the pack.

11. Generally, there are two ways to evaluate the ambition level of upstarts (young, aspiring professionals): (1) those that talk about their motivation, focus, and drive and (2) those that execute their plans based on their motivation, focus, and ambition.

12. It is no secret that many of us covet success, prestige, respect, and status. The problem is many of us are not willing to do whatever it takes to achieve the things that we covet.

13. At all cost, avoid airing dirty laundry in meetings. Before the meeting is where the real decisions are made.

The "Strive for Excellence" Operating System

The "Strive for Excellence" Operating System

Perfection is unattainable; striving for excellence is achievable. Excellence is giving every assigned task your best effort. Why settle for a 3.0 when you are capable of making a 4.0? Many of us baby boomers recall our parents warning us of the importance of the family name. Don't misrepresent the family name! Your stamp of excellence is similar to representing the family name. It's the brand that is attached to your work. Every task you perform is a reflection of you. Everything you do will have your name on it (your personal brand). You will be associated either with mediocrity or either excellence. Don't assume that there is a middle ground.

> *Many people confuse perfection with striving for excellence. Excellence is demonstrated by your desire to do the absolute best you can at any assigned task, no matter how big, small, or mundane the task is.*

We are what we repeatedly do; excellence then is not an act, but a habit.
— Aristotle

Attention-to-Detail—When you account for or take care of the small tasks, rarely will you be caught off guard by the suddenness of an unexpected larger task. In other words, take care of the small things, and the larger things will take care of themselves. Omitting small tasks can create the need to address larger tasks. As an example, when you fail to change the oil in your car (a small task), you may have to buy a new engine (a big task). Sometimes laboring in daily, operational tasks can become mundane and monotonous. But no matter how dull it may appear, you must continue to take care of the business at hand.

The key to being able to place continuous emphasis on attention to detail is having a proactive mindset. Many of us are reactive when responding to work-related situations or events, rather than being proactive. Depending on the type of business you are working in, being reactive rather than proactive may not be good enough. A proactive approach requires that you are continuously and consistently planning, evaluating, monitoring, anticipating, checking, and adjusting to cover your duties and responsibilities. Attention to detail can prevent waste, loss of time and effort (productivity), and loss of money. It even can prevent embarrassment. It also enhances safety and affects morale positively.

Focusing on attention to detail applies equally to employees, managers and supervisors.

Implied Task—What is an implied task? It is a job assignment; action, chore, or undertaking that is suggested and understood without being expressed directly. When executed, an implied task is usually positive and will ultimately support a larger, more strategic function.

Comprehending exactly how executing implied tasks enhance the overall work environment is a bonus to your company or organization as well as to your career. Organizational benefits include getting the job done with minimal directives and less-detailed instructions or communications. Managers and supervisors value employees who do not have to be told how and when to do everything. When they don't have to micromanage every detail of your working life, managers and supervisors are freed up to concentrate on high-priority tasks.

An implied task can be a small, subtle undertaking or it can be a large, seldom-required major task. To excel at executing implied tasks, it's beneficial to have a good concept of tactical and strategic thinking and comprehension; in addition to having understanding, insightfulness, and attentiveness.

Executing business plans that are created at the executive management level and executed at the business or operating unit level requires a high degree of good judgment. It also is a good illustration of how implied tasks work on a broader scale. Executives think strategically, and employees operate on a tactical (day-to-day) level. The business or operating unit is required to take the strategic plan and create business or operating unit goals that will sustain, support, and enhance all the strategic goals and objectives.

For example, if one of the themes within the executive business plan is to "elevate customer service to the best in class category," it is surely the responsibility of the business or operating unit manager to return to his or her business or operating unit and conduct an internal assessment to determine if there are any customer service-related deviations from standards issues under his or her direct operational control that may require additional resources or an action plan to ultimately improve on. With this approach, what is important at the executive leadership level is also emphasized at the operating unit level.

Another example of an implied task on a more tactical level is my interaction with my senior office assistant. She fully understands that I place great emphasis on meetings and timeliness. So when a meeting invitation comes by e-mail, I should not have to remind her about initiating scheduling coordination and planning; she should, without hesitation, do that without me having to say anything. Without guidance and whenever required, my senior office assistant ensures that all requirements are thoroughly coordinated.

What's important to your boss should be important to you. Bosses should not have to remind their employees every time they feel that something is important to them. Implied tasks are not assigned; they are assumed and anticipated.

The Subject Matter Expert—This is the employee who has the tools, knowledge, skills, and technical expertise in a particular job or field. Technical expertise is gained through formal education, extensive study, institutional knowledge, on-the-job training, a pursuit of excellence, dedication, and a commitment to a particular specialty.

Why is there so much importance attached to becoming a subject matter expert? The people who are able to position themselves as subject matter experts typically are on the fast track to promotions, status, power, authority, leadership, and increased responsibility. This lofty status is not for everyone. In fact, many who aspire to achieve this level of proficiency don't achieve it. There is no definitive timetable associated with becoming a subject matter expert, but no one does it overnight.

If you have subject matter expertise, you are valued. Managers and supervisors depend on you. During your employment, strive to attain subject matter expertise in your job.

Success is generated by having the right people doing the right jobs at the right time with the right skill set. This is a key to resolving a company's or an organization's problems. Becoming a subject matter expert is more about your internal drive, personal motivation, and values than anything else. It's the intangibles that really make a difference.

You're not obligated to win. You're obligated to keep trying to do the best you can every day.
— Marian Wright Edelman

Preparing for a Presentation—I honestly can't remember exactly when I gave my first presentation in front of others. I'm guessing that I had already reached young adulthood, or perhaps my first presentation was connected with a church activity. In contrast, I can recall my daughters preparing for oral team presentations as early as elementary school during the late 1990s. In the school system that my children were educated in, oral presentations were routine.

Clearly, in today's working environment, the probability of you having to give some type of oral presentation early in your career is very real. Don't confuse oral presentations with the ability to debate others or with Public Speaking 101. You need to have the ability to give a professional, work-related presentation via PowerPoint, video conferencing, and a face-to-face briefing.

A checklist has been provided to assist you in this endeavor. But first, allow me to reiterate a few key points noted or implied in the checklist:

- Familiarity or thorough knowledge of the subject matter is key; this can't be overemphasized.

The "Strive for Excellence" Operating System

- One difference-maker in delivering your presentation is knowing whether or not you will be limited to a podium or a platform rather than having the freedom to move around.
- Practice really does make perfect.
- Prepare short notes to keep you on point.
- Bouncing your ideas off a trusted confidant is a definite plus.
- Synchronize or coordinate handouts where appropriate.
- Anticipate the tough questions; in fact, an indicator of a well-put-together presentation is when there are few questions at the end of it.
- Use a voice and/or tone that support a clear and concise style of delivery.
- Don't psyche yourself out.
- Be you.

Remember, there is simply no substitute for being professionally prepared.

Checklist
Preparing for a Presentation

	Task List	Comments/Notes
1	Research your topic.	
2	Gather resources.	
3	Develop your presentation. Does it flow? Check spelling, punctuation, and grammar.	
4	Plan and practice.	
5	Know your audience.	
6	Anticipate the tough questions.	
7	Be well groomed.	
8	Select your attire.	
9	Secure the proper equipment: laptop, projector, screen and pointer.	
10	If possible, visit the presentation site in advance.	
11	Identify power outlets, light switches, lighting, room temperature controls, and so on.	
12	Be on time.	
13	Conduct an advance function check on your equipment.	
14	Distribute copies of the presentation or handouts, if appropriate.	
15	Ease into it. Start with a lighthearted intro.	
16	Adhere to time constraints.	

Know What the Standards Are—Companies and organizations communicate their expectations by establishing workplace standards. Once you secure a job, it is critical for you to determine what is expected of you as an employee. There are standards or expectations for the position that you were hired to fill, and there are standards and expectations for the company or organization as a whole.

Standards are like milestones or benchmarks that determine whether or not you are doing things the way you are supposed to be doing them. Standards are the blueprints or the templates for doing what you do. Why are establishing standards so important? They clarify expectations. Standards define the who, what, when, where, and why of things. Standards might be discussed in an employee orientation setting, or they might be discussed one on one with your manager or supervisor.

First, let's explore company or organizational standards. These are communicated via the mission and vision statements, employee code of conduct, various policies, and operating procedures. After being hired, make it a priority to find out and review all the company or organizational standards. Once you are made aware of the standards, you will be held accountable to adhering to those standards. Company or organizational standards will vary, depending on the company and its culture.

Second, job-related standards are communicated via performance appraisals, job descriptions, and position score cards. Your continued employment will be determined by how well you achieve these stated goals. A sample Senior Office Assistant Score Card is provided on the next page.

To operate at an optimum level, you must first fully understand what the company's or organization's standards or expectations are. Also, to remain on point, periodically review your job-related and company or organizational standards. At any time during your employment, if you fail to achieve or sustain expectations, your manager or supervisor will surely make you aware of your shortcomings. Ignorance will not suffice as an excuse for not knowing exactly what is expected of you individually and collectively.

Sample Score Card
Senior Office Assistant
Customer Service Support Team/ABC Inc.

Mission

The Office Assistant for ABC Inc. provides effective administrative support for the Customer Service Support Team. Under the supervision of the Manager, the senior office assistant assists in the coordination of office management and operational activities by performing varied clerical tasks as assigned. Interaction involves routine information exchange and/or simple service activity that require common courtesy; e.g., directing calls, and answering simple questions. Overall level of performance is expected to enhance the Customer Service Support Team's ability to function as a "high performance organization."

Outcomes

- Customer assistance is provided to a 95% satisfactory rating to support the company's overall mission, purpose, and vision.
- Must perform 100% of all duties and responsibilities autonomously, with the Manager available to answer questions as they arise.
- Directly manages calendars, meetings, agendas, and travel arrangements for the Manager with minimal (10% or <) oversight.
- With minimal error (10% or <), ensures the quality and distribution of all internal and outbound correspondence to support the team's goals.
- Must maintain files and office supplies to prescribed company standards
- Demonstrate proficiency (through an HR administered test) with all standardized computer programs, e.g., MS Word, MS PowerPoint, MS Excel, MS Outlook, and other applicable company-specific i.e. SAP, and requisition computer programs.

The "Strive for Excellence" Operating System

Competencies

- Confidentiality
- Excellence—sets an exemplary example
- Trustworthy
- Attention to detail
- Problem solver
- Dependable
- Proactive

_____   _____
Employee's Signature   Supervisor's Signature

_____
Date

Team Building—Successful team building requires the ability to assess and evaluate talent. Let me remind you that team building is not easy. There is no exact science to forming a team, but there are many criteria and considerations that go into selecting team members that will ultimately support your company's or organization's mission, vision, and philosophy.

In general, good teams possess the following attributes.

1. Adaptability

Good team members are adaptable to one another and they understand synergy. The individuals on a good team know each other very well and know it is important to be flexible with one another. Each person is unique. All of us have different ideas, opinions, and beliefs. Good team members understand that it is extremely important to meet the needs of the team as a whole and learn to accept ideas that are different from their own. As a result, a team is a cohesive unit. Individual team members don't make a big deal over their small differences and constantly focus on assigned goal.

2. Enthusiasm

Good teams have high energy. They are comprised of enthusiastic members, and each member provides energy to the others. When a team has low energy, it draws on the negativity of its members. People feel tired after being with a group of unenthusiastic people. Good teams attract people into the group because of their high energy level. People want to be part of a team with enthusiasm.

3. Vision

Vision is one of the most important characteristics of a good team. Good teams stay focused on their goals; they rarely lose their focus on their purpose for coming together. A good team or organization never loses site of its purpose.

4. Selflessness

A good team learns the importance of being selfless. Members of a good team understand the importance of the organizational vision versus their personal vision. The members of a good team understand the value of identifying each other's strength and weaknesses.

5. Commitment

A good team understands the importance of being committed to a single cause—in this case, the vision of the team or organization. Commitment often means that team members do things despite inconveniences and distractions.

6. Good Communication with One Another

A good team understands the importance of clear and concise communications with one another. Constant communication means that obstacles and distractions are eliminated and misunderstandings are minimized. By keeping the channels of communications open, team members are able to remain supportive of one another.

How to Handle Delegation—Delegation is very much a part of normal business activity, interactive management, and leadership. There are different criteria for the person doing the delegating versus the person who is on the receiving end of the delegation process.

No one person can do everything. To be successful, you must be able to understand the dynamics of delegation. As the delegator, if you simply assign the task to others without clarity, guidance, standards, authority, or accountability, you are likely to fail. Also, mere delegation does not always cut it. Not only must you assess or evaluate the task or assignment being delegated, you must also assess the capabilities of the person the task or assignment is delegated to. Ensuring ample time and resources are also key.

Periodically, you may want to check on the progress of the delegated assignment. If help, resources, or additional guidance is needed, you will be able to offer your input before being presented with a finished product that does not meet established standards. Make sure deadlines are clear.

The recipient of the delegated task has a different set of criteria to be concerned about. What do you do if an assigned task is beyond your capability? Do you voice your concerns? Do you rely on other resources? Do you simply accept the assignment and place all bets on your ability to complete the assigned task adequately? There is no magic formula in determining the answers to these questions. How you respond to accepting an assigned task depends on you. Be honest. You should find a balance or comfort zone between accepting a challenge and being in over your head. Remember, acceptance implies ownership. More importantly, if you encounter difficulties or a delay, it is absolutely crucial that you communicate your concerns to the person who assigned you the task. Missing a deadline is unacceptable.

Timelines, deadlines, and deliverables apply equally to everyone up and down the chain of command. Your position in the chain in regard to delegation is not the issue. The issue is, no matter where you fit, do not become the weak link by failing to complete an assigned task.

Critical Points of Emphasis:
The "Strive for Excellence" Operating System

1. The key to being able to adapt to a style that emphasizes attention to detail is having a proactive mindset.

2. Managers and supervisors value employees who do not have to be told how and when to do everything.

3. What's important to your boss should be important to you.

4. The people who are able to position themselves as subject matter experts typically are on the fast track to promotions, status, power, authority, leadership, and increased responsibility.

5. Once you secure a job, it's critical for you to determine what is expected of you as an employee.

6. To operate at an optimum level, you must first fully understand what the company's or organization's standards or expectations are.

7. Missing a deadline is unacceptable.

8. Standards are like milestones or benchmarks that determine whether or not you are doing things the way you are supposed to be doing them.

9. Implied tasks are not assigned; they are assumed.

10. Every task you perform is a reflection of you.

11. Good team members understand that it is extremely important to be flexible in order to meet the needs of the team as a whole and learn to accept ideas that are different from their own.

12. Constant communication means that obstacles and distractions are eliminated and misunderstandings are minimized.

E⁵ Theory

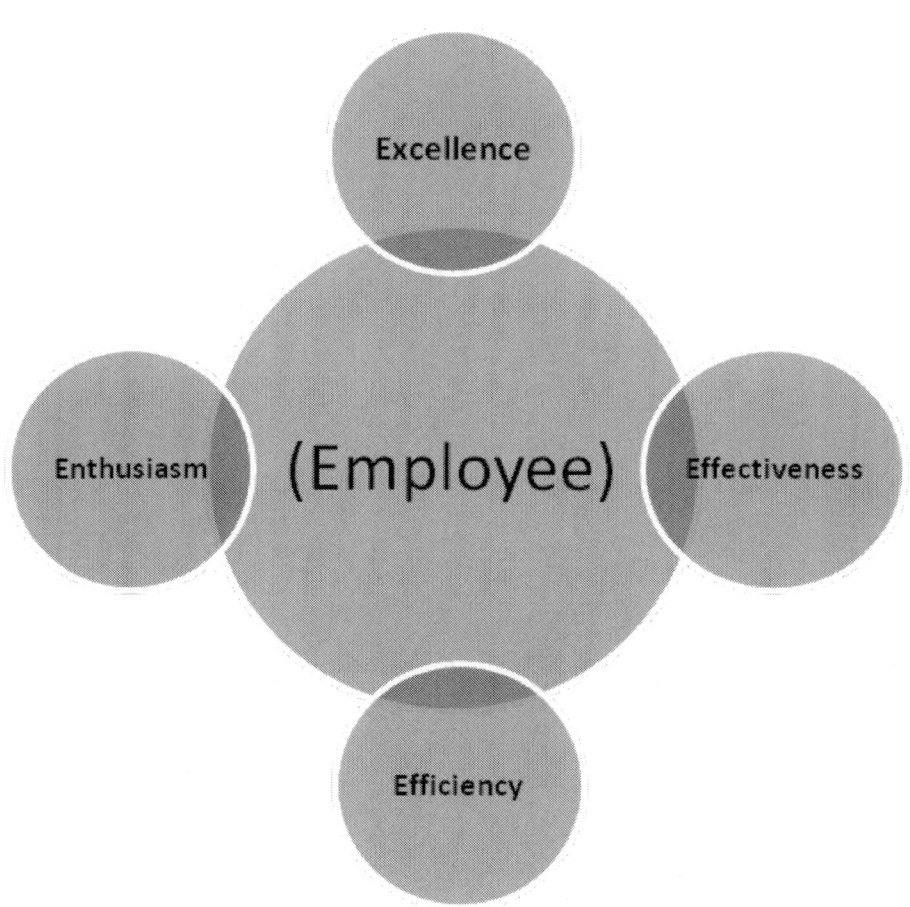

Companies and organizations accomplish their mission, vision, priorities, goals, and objectives through people: their employees. When effectiveness and efficiency are combined with enthusiasm, the result is a conduit that produces or unleashes an employee who performs at his or her optimum potential. That plateau of optimum potential is where excellence resides. An efficient, effective, and enthusiastic employee who operates in excellence is the desired template. Real enthusiasm is influenced by internal (self-motivating) factors and external (leader-influenced) factors. Often employee enthusiasm is the most overlooked of the five components.

The Action Gap

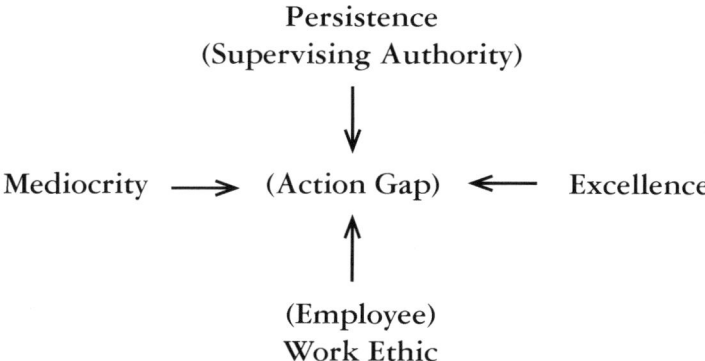

An action gap (what employees can do versus what employees will do) exists between an employee's attitude of mediocrity (complacency or apathy) and attitude of excellence. To overcome this deficiency, this action gap requires action on the part of the individual employee (work ethic) and the responsible supervising authority (persistence). The longer the action gap is ignored, the more difficult closing the gap becomes. Note: The negative impact of mediocrity is often overlooked or downplayed by both the employer and employee. An employee's work ethic combined with persistence to perform at expected levels of competency minimizes or eliminates the action Gap. Someone must take action—either the employee or the supervising authority.

The "Embrace Technology" Operating System

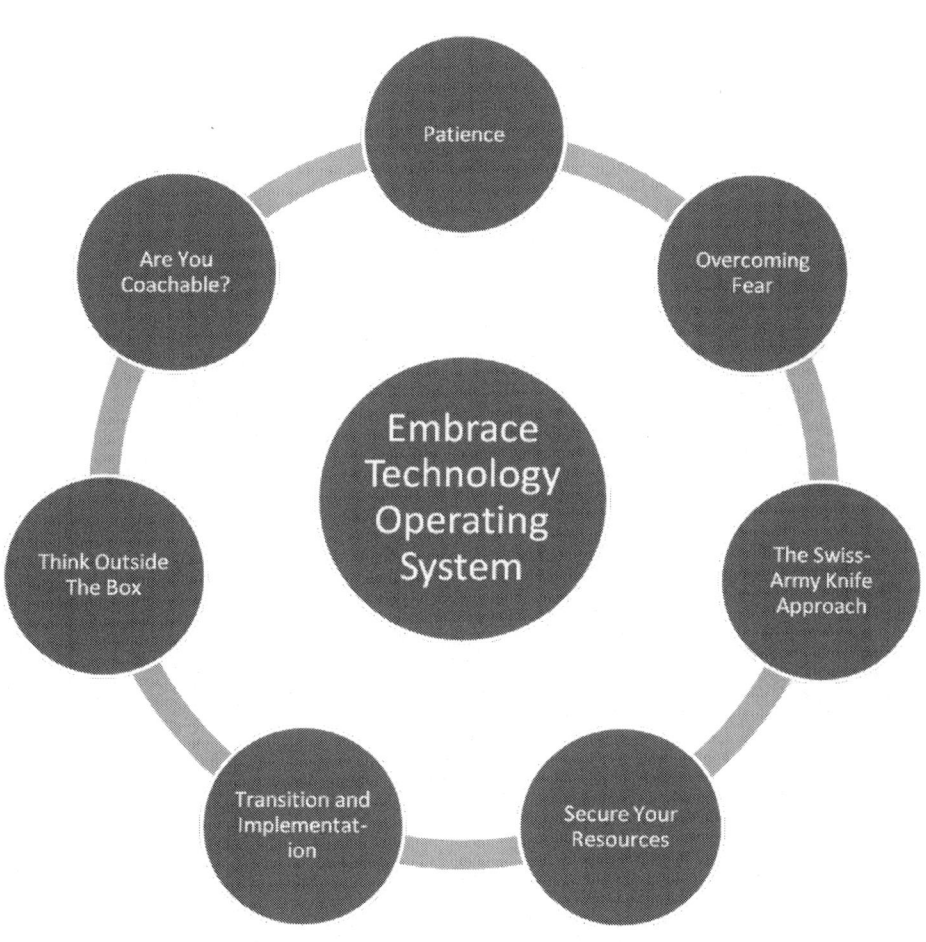

The "Embrace Technology" Operating System

Today, its iPhones, iPads, GPS, satellite radio, smartphones, OnStar, digital technology, WiFi, and PCs in nearly every classroom and home. What will it be tomorrow? I can remember one of my instructors in the seventies telling us that one day computers would dominate society. Back then, we all laughed at such a wild assertion. Today, there is the possibility of prototype flying cars. I don't laugh at technological assertions today like I did back in the seventies. Technology is moving so swiftly that some advances are almost obsolete by the time they hit the consumer market. The world around us is technology driven. Embrace it or risk being on the outside looking in. Failure to embrace it will almost surely relegate you to the abyss (a low-level, no-tech, low-paying job).

> *The future of technology is now; either you embrace it or it will pass you by.*

You gain strength, courage, and confidence by every experience in which you really stop to look fear in the face. You must do the thing which you think you cannot do.
— Eleanor Roosevelt

Overcoming Fear—It does not matter what type of fear you are attempting to overcome; realize that at some point you are going to have to confront that fear. I decided to discuss overcoming fear in this chapter because new technology is intimidating for many of us. While overcoming fear is being discussed here, by no means is overcoming fear limited to this topic. Nor do I want to imply that it is.

Everyone recognizes that very little positivity ever comes out of being fearful. First and foremost, as we mature, we need to get beyond things in life that inhibit us. Fear in the workplace keeps you from performing at your maximum potential.

Preparedness, practice, developing self-confidence, working on building up low self-esteem, accepting small or incremental challenges, and confiding in someone you trust can all help you to overcome fear. Initially, it may not appear easy, particularly if you are a new employee facing new challenges.

At one point early in my career, I was terrified of public speaking. I knew in the back of my mind that as I continued to advance and take on more responsibility, at some point I had to overcome this deficiency. How did I do it? I gathered all the available resources. I studied the material until I became comfortable with it. I consulted with a colleague who was experienced in giving presentations. I practiced in front of my wife; when she wasn't available, I used a mirror. Once it was time for my presentation, I was honest with my audience about my nervousness. They in return were very considerate and understanding. In the end, it all went well; I actually made it through. And it wasn't as bad as I had made it out to be. Each time I repeated this process, I became more comfortable with each presentation.

Conduct a self-assessment of your fears. Then work on overcoming those fears. The key is to have the courage to try. If you stumble, I assure that it is not the end of the world. People often stumble. Learn from your misstep and keep moving forward.

Whatever your fears may be, the potential danger is to relax once you reach a certain level of comfort and expertise. When attempting to overcome fear, often the greatest obstacle is the failure to try.

The greatest barrier to success is the fear of failure.
— Sven Goran Eriksson

The Swiss-Army Knife Approach—Every Boy Scout, hunter, fisherman, outdoors-person, handyman, and soldier appreciates having a good Swiss Army pocket knife on hand. The original Swiss Army knife is the most functional multi-tool on the market. It has a blade and various others tools, such as a screwdriver and a can opener. The term "Swiss-Army knife" has entered popular culture as a metaphor for usefulness and adaptability. The design of the knife and its flexibility has led to recognition worldwide.

The ideal work situation is when we are able to focus on a single task at a time and at our own pace. This rarely happens in the real world. Much like the Swiss Army knife, skills in multitasking and functioning in various skills and at various levels are needed in this busy world if you are to survive.

There are differences of professional opinions about the value of multifunctional and multitasking skills. An opposing opinion is that if you focus on doing several tasks well, you'll never be great at any of them. It doesn't matter which opinion you prefer, because one thing is certain: employers value employees who can fill in and perform wherever and whenever necessary. This approach can positively affect your company's or organization's contingency plan as well as support cost-saving measures.

There is a direct link between these skills and the "Embrace Technology" Operating System. Technology is a primary tool or resource, enabling you to enhance your capabilities.

In some professional classifications, multifunctional and multitasking skills are a competency of the job. For example, a communications center specialist is required to provide customer service, answer the telephone, respond to base radio calls, respond to emergencies, and do data entry.

You could be assigned multiple tasks with multiple deadlines and multiple projects. You and only you know what you can and what you cannot shoulder. You may also face the fear of appearing wimpy if you complain. When or if you find yourself in this situation, honesty, prioritizing, time management, preparation, doing it right the first time, and the proper use of resources are essential.

Secure Your Resources—Having to work within the boundaries of existing resources or having to secure non-existing resources is a harsh reality. The method by which resources are obtained varies from company to company based on the nature, size, duration, scope, cost, and importance of the project or task you are involved in. A general resource checklist may involve the following:

1. Identify the needs (staff, financial, and technical resources).
2. Develop a budget to support, implement, and evaluate a plan.
3. Integrate the assessment plan with the organization's processes.
4. Identify existing resources.
5. Identify potential external funding resources.
6. Secure identified resources.
7. Consider options and develop alternatives.

It doesn't matter how large or small your project is: resources should be considered. Where possible, try to resolve your resource issues up front. By doing so, you are free to focus on the project itself rather than worry about resource-related issues.

Transition and Implementation—As technology continues to advance, it will become increasingly important for you to keep pace with technological advances. The competition for increased production, customer demand, and rising expectations is on the rise. Technology, and employees' ability to keep pace with it, is critical to your company or organization, just as it is to each employee. People need proper education and training if they're expected to accomplish the majority of their work; nowhere is this more evident than with technology.

Today's employee must enter the workplace ready to make an immediate contribution. You will need to develop and sustain your abilities in keyboarding, MS Word, Excel, and PowerPoint. Many companies and organizations also have rolled out company-specific programs,

The "Embrace Technology" Operating System

such as Share Point, SAP, intranet, and payroll, budget, and logistical applications.

Decisions to purchase new technology are carefully considered by individual companies and organizations. Technology is only a tool, and it doesn't replace effective management. After the decision to purchase the technology has been made, it is time to focus on implementation. It is essential to understand the factors that may make employees hesitant to embrace the new technology. People have problems embracing new technology because human nature itself often resists change. Also, some people have a basic fear of technology; it's simply intimidating. When technology's benefits are clearly demonstrated to employees, they are more likely to embrace a new system. Training is really a two-step process—it's not just formal training, but you also need a core group of internal employees within the organization that can champion the new system and help other employees use it.

Tech savviness is a weighty precondition for hiring. Employees who use technology outside of work—a home computer, for example—are often more comfortable embracing technology at work. Companies look for basic comfort and familiarity with technology. Because the use of technology is so essential to every company's operating system, people who reject technological change and implementation are not hired.

Systems, processes, techniques, technology, and people are always evolving and changing. As these things occur all around you, you must have the disposition to be able to effectively and efficiently cope with transition.

Think Outside the Box—What is gained from employees who think outside the box? An atmosphere is established that encourages workplace creativity, motivating employees, sparking new ideas, and boosting the bottom line.

Companies and organizations are keenly aware that the current generation of employees generally doesn't stay at ho-hum companies where nothing changes, creativity is discouraged, and innovation is stifled. Think outside the box in terms of how you can do your part to help serve clients and become part of a staff that is recognized as being among the best. Be flexible and show autonomy; this will help create an environment that makes everyone feel more relaxed and innovative.

Companies that give their employees autonomy are often the most successful at stirring innovation. Companies are not looking for children to raise. If you are able to convince your employer that you are capable of working in an environment that promotes more autonomy, you will promote a feeling of trust, which ultimately inspires greater motivation and productivity in everyone. Employees whose ideas are quickly dismissed are going to get irritated and probably not work hard to be innovative the next time

I was working at a facility that was looking to expand its commercial transportation loading zones. Because the facility was essentially landlocked, there appeared to be no room for expansion. In addition to being landlocked, the facility was thirty-plus years old. Commercial loading zones and thoroughfares for ingress and egress to and from the facility were overused and had some traffic-flow restrictions. We were able to identify a very large, unused concrete island that was big enough to accommodate up to three very large commercial transporters while meeting all associated restrictions. This piece of real estate had been unused and ignored for as long as the facility had been there. We were able to help secure funding from the primary user. We were also able to secure buy-in from management and all collaborative parties. The project was a win-win-win for the organization, its commercial transportation providers, and their customers.

The ability to think outside the box is a valued skill set for any employee. Smart managers and supervisors know that the best resource to improve a product, process, idea, or work flow is often through the innovative eyes of the people who actually perform daily on the front line.

It may be advantageous for you to offer a different perspective, background, or level of expertise to create some good tension. Again, companies and organizations know that if you are happy, you'll be more relaxed at work, more likely to be innovative, and more invested in creating the best company possible. Engaged employees takes ownership. They love their job and love their life, and they want both to always get better.

You can't make someone work hard; they have to choose to do that. As an employee, you can help create an environment where people are likely to be productive and innovative.

Minds are like parachutes; they work best when open.
- T. Dewar

Are You Coachable ?—I have often heard that when you arrive at a point on the job where you feel you can no longer learn from someone, it is time for you to hang it up and move on. When you experience this, remember that this mindset affects not only you but also others.

To remain successful in dealing with workplace demands, performance improvements, and increased productivity, you must become coachable. And, as previously stated, you don't know everything. So the question that is begging to be answered is, are you coachable?

For the sake of clarity, mentoring is a relational process in which a mentor, who knows or has experienced something (resources of wisdom, information, experience, confidence, insight, relationship, and status), transfers that something to a mentee at an appropriate time and manner, so that it facilitates development and empowerment. But coaching is an ongoing professional relationship that helps people produce extraordinary results in their lives, careers, businesses, or organizations. Through the process of coaching, employees deepen their understanding, improve their performance, and enhance their productivity. In each meeting or call, the coach listens and contributes observations and questions. This interaction creates clarity and moves the employee into effective action.

Mentoring	Coaching
You decide on your mentor	Your job determines your coach
Focuses on the personal and professional	Focuses on the professional
Timing is self-determined	Timing is determined by your coach
Frequency is determined by you	Frequency is determined by your coach
No risk of disciplinary actions	Could result in disciplinary action
Interactions are congenial	Congeniality may not be applicable
Results in personal goals being reached	Results in increased productivity

Why Coach?

- Training alone is never enough to create optimal performance.
- Employees need to increase their performance level.

- To manage all the changes required while executing daily duties and responsibilities.
- To help focus on what's important.
- To help reduce stress.
- To retain top talent and boost employee morale, enabling success. So rather than waiting for things to go wrong or accepting subpar performance, it's important that employees receive ongoing performance feedback, or coaching.

What are the company-related benefits of coaching?

- Overcome costly and time-consuming performance problems.
- Strengthen employees' skills so you can delegate more tasks and focus on more important managerial responsibilities.
- Boost productivity by helping your employees work smarter.
- Develop bench strength among the team.
- Improve retention; employees are more loyal and motivated when their manager or supervisor takes the time to help improve their skills.
- Make more effective use of company resources; coaching costs less than formal training.

When you're an employee being coached, you

- build valuable skills and knowledge that can be used to advance your career,
- feel supported and encouraged by your manager and company, and
- experience the pride and satisfaction that comes with surmounting new challenges.

What you learn determines how much you earn.

Patience—It is often said that patience is a virtue. Patience is also an asset. It is the ability to sit back and wait for an expected outcome without experiencing anxiety, tension, or frustration. It is the ability to let go of your need for immediate gratification and to wait. Patience is the ability to remain calm, no matter what obstacles you face.

When I think about patience, again, I think back to my days as an up-and-coming basketball official. Basketball officiating is very competitive. Training is demanding. Evaluations and constructive criticism are a way of life. Attending officiating clinics to better your skills is routine. Everyone wants to position himself or herself for that big televised or playoff game. Within the business, we had a saying: "It's better to be a day too late rather than a day too early." You can be so eager to get that big game that when you finally do get the opportunity, you blow it because you weren't ready like you thought you were. Bottom line, you were elevated too soon. If this were to occur, not only would you be exposed but you could also incur irreversible career damage. Being elevated too soon can destroy everything you've worked for. There is nothing more humbling than public failure.

Another example of the need to be patient is deeply rooted in my memory. Somewhere around 1983, I had my first automobile accident in which I was at fault. An older gentleman was in front of me, waiting to make a right turn into the flow of traffic. As I sat impatiently behind him, he missed what I thought were several opportunities to make the turn and merge into traffic. In my haste to go, I turned my head, saw that there was a large enough gap for the driver in front of me to go, and pressed the accelerator to make the right turn. Well, the car was still there, and I crashed into it from behind. Clearly it was my fault; all I needed was a little more patience and the accident could have been avoided.

Well, twenty-nine years later, I found myself in the exact same situation, waiting to make a right turn onto the feeder road adjacent to the freeway, sitting behind a car that was reluctant to enter traffic and make the same right turn. Wouldn't you know it, history repeated itself? I had my second at-fault automobile accident when I crashed into the rear of the vehicle in front of me. The very first thought that came to my mind was the accident twenty-nine years earlier. I asked myself, *Haven't you learned anything about patience in twenty-nine years?* As I absorbed the reality of what had just occurred, my answer was *Patience is a process*.

Fortunately, these accidents weren't devastating. No one was injured, and I was able to accept fault and continue on with life. Developing patience is truly a process. Learning to be more tolerant of others and recognizing personal shortcomings is a good place to start. As you engage others in the workplace, you will be challenged to develop patience. Hopefully, the process you endure will not take as long as it took for me.

When everything is going our way, patience is easy to demonstrate. The true test of patience comes when our rights are violated—when another car cuts us off in traffic; when we are treated unfairly; when our coworkers don't see or do things the way we think they should. Some people think they have a right to get upset in the face of irritations and trials. Patience does not develop overnight. The next time you are in a traffic jam, frustrated by a coworker, mad at your boss, or frustrated because your career is not advancing fast enough, how will you respond? The natural response is impatience, which leads to stress, anger, frustration, and other side effects.

Critical Points of Emphasis:
The "Embrace Technology" Operating System

1. Failure to embrace technology will almost surely relegate you to the abyss (a low-level, no-tech, low-paying job).

2. Very little positivity ever comes out of being fearful, yet when it's time to take action to overcome fear, people often feel powerless.

3. Try to resolve your resource issues up front. By doing so, you are free to focus on the project itself rather than worrying about resource-related issues.

4. People need proper education and training if they are to accomplish the majority of their work; nowhere is this more evident than with technology.

5. Be flexible and show autonomy; this will help create an environment that makes everyone else feel more relaxed and innovative.

6. If you are able to convince your employer that you are capable of working in an environment that promotes autonomy, you will promote a feeling of trust, which ultimately inspires greater motivation and productivity in everyone.

7. An engaged employee takes ownership.

8. To remain successful in dealing with transition, change, flexibility, and versatility, you must become coachable.

9. Employers value employees who have the ability to multitask.

10. Through the process of coaching, employees deepen their learning, improve their performance, and enhance their productivity.

11. You can't make people work hard; they have to choose to do so. As an employee, you can help create an environment where people are likely to be productive and innovative.

12. In regard to advancing your career, it is better to be a day too late than a day too early.

13. Developing patience is truly a process. Learning to be more tolerant of others and recognizing personal shortcomings is a good place to start.

The "Be Adaptable to Change" Operating System

The "Be Adaptable to Change" Operating System

Change involves a process of generating a new idea, accepting it, implementing it, responding to conflict, and making what was once new part of the routine. Change is inevitable. Change and adapting to changes are a part of life.

Many of us do not really like change. How many times have you heard, "We've been doing it this way for years? Why do they want to change it now?" Why is it that so many people loathe change? Is it fear? Does change require you to abandon your comfort zone? Is it because of insecurity? Is it complacency?

> *Dissatisfaction and discouragement are not caused by the absence of things but by the absence of vision. Vision requires change.*

When we are no longer able to change a situation, we are challenged to change ourselves.
— Victor Frank

Prioritizing and Shifting Priorities—Prioritizing skills allow you to focus on what is most important. Learn to set priorities wisely, and you will achieve more and will have more personal or family time at your disposal. How well or poorly you prioritize the different needs in your life will affect almost everything you do, every decision you make. You will reap tremendous gains if you are able to properly prioritize your day-to-day work activities.

Prioritizing can help you be organized. It brings order to chaos. If you are unable to prioritize your daily activities while at work, you will operate in an unstable work environment. What is important to your company or organization? What should you be focusing on to meet your assigned goals? If there are multiple goals, which one has a higher precedence? How does timing affect your priorities? What is important to your boss? Do you have too many priorities? What is the potential impact if you prioritize incorrectly?

You must evaluate your list of priorities very carefully. When done properly, prioritizing requires you to know the answers to these tough questions. Prioritizing requires that you have an in-depth understanding of exactly what is expected of you. It also requires you to be disciplined and committed as well as to understand timeliness and the impact of missed deadlines.

As a manager, I have often established a priority list at the end of the day in preparation for the next day. The problem is, once I arrive at the office the next day, reality sometimes wins out over the priority list. I quickly realized that I had to attain a balance between my priorities and unanticipated distractions.

Why prioritize? You prioritize to

- work smarter, not harder;
- improve on time management;
- enhances work flow;
- promote efficiency and effectiveness;
- create a should-do list, nice-to-do list, and a must-do list;
- have a clear understanding of what your "deliverables" are;
- use your online organizer wisely, including calendars, task lists, reminders, alerts, and files; and
- eliminate clutter.

It is not uncommon for priorities to shift frequently. When this occurs, you must be able to make adjustments. Shifting priorities in the workplace are a way of life, because the modern-day work environment is fast paced and challenging. Working in this kind of environment can be an eye opener. You must be able to balance shifting priorities, period. The reality is management has unanticipated deadlines and shifting priorities as well. When situations like this occur, you must be able to adapt.

You may not have to endure the shifting priorities of a manager, but shifting priorities are likely to be a daily challenge at work. Depending on the nature of your work, these shifts may vary in regard to intensity. When and if this occurs, you can't allow yourself to become flustered. To excel in this area, your ability to focus, work hard, utilize appropriate resources, plan, and prepare will help you to cope.

In all likelihood, the more you are challenged in this area, the more confidence you will gain.

Goals and Vision—A goal is a specific commitment to achieve a measurable result within a given timeframe. Goals are critical stepping stones, benchmarks, or measurable outcomes necessary to achieve a purpose. They identify whether you or your team are going in the right direction, how well you or your team are doing, and how you or your team will know when you get there. Goals tell all employees what they are trying to accomplish or improve on, reveal if you are on a desired path, determines measurements, targeted outcomes , and provide targets dates for completion. Goals can be tactical or strategic. They can be short term, intermediate, or long term. They should be smart, measurable, attainable, relevant, trackable, and timely. The vision required to set goals in business helps identify a path, direction, and destination for future accomplishments.

What affect do goals and vision have on individual employees? They outline the who, what, when, where, and how of the company or organization. You should know how your job contributes to the overall success, productivity, branding, and profitability of your company or organization. Believe it or not, there is a reason you do whatever it is you're getting paid to do.

Flexibility—Reluctance or resistance to change can place you in a vice grip-like state of mind. One of the surest ways to overcome this vice grip is to focus on being flexible. You may say, "Easier said than done." Well, most things in life that is worth accomplishing are not easy.

The work environment is under a constant state of flux, particularly now. If you deal with people, and most of us do, the simple fact that your company requires you to provide a service or produce a product puts you on the fast track of dealing with clients and customers. And as long as there are clients and customers, there will be a need to understand the effect of being flexible in whatever you do. People are diverse. You must possess or learn the skills to be flexible enough to handle all the challenges associated with diversity.

Flexibility pertains not only to dealing with people; it also applies to the ability to be versatile on the job. Switching from one task to another requires flexibility. Mastering a different system or process requires flexibility. Coping with changing priorities requires flexibility. Changing leadership requires flexibility.

To better understand the human complexities of the work environment, see the "Generations and Their Characteristics" on page 141.

The reasonable man adapts himself to the world; the unreasonable one persists in trying to adapt the world to himself. Therefore all progress depends on the unreasonable man.

- George Bernard Shaw

Understand the Value of Assessments—Honest assessments in any business unit, whether internal or external, are a pathway to sustaining excellence. Early in my first career as a flight operations chief, I stumbled on the benefits of conducting self-generated, internal assessments. Flight operation is an administrative challenge. Overseeing this area requires knowledge and training in meteorology, flight planning, interoperability with other agencies, deciphering aeronautical charts, and many other meticulous tasks. In the event of an aircraft mishap, flight operations requirements are gone over with a fine-tooth comb. In this environment, overlooked tasks can create a cascading effect.

To keep from being overwhelmed and to increase efficiency, I implemented a very detailed and honest internal assessment every quarter. We took a checklist that was initially used by external auditors, added our institutional knowledge, and retooled the checklist to add value to our operations. This approach provided us with tremendous results. It became routine for us to receive exceptional ratings on major external inspections. After leaving the military, I took this same approach to the civilian sector, and to this day, it has resulted in high-end results.

When you perform a task right the first time, the need for internal assessments decrease and efficiency increases.

Strategic Thinking—Strategic thinking is connected to vision. It is broad, involving a grasp of the big picture. Strategic thinking formulates effective strategies consistent with the business and competitive strategy of a company or organization in a global economy. Strategic thinking examines policy issues and strategic planning with a long-term perspective; determines objectives and sets priorities; and anticipates potential threats and opportunities.

Strategic thinking is typically associated with senior or executive managers. But it is advantageous for non-senior managers or non-executives to at least be familiar with the significance of strategic thinking. Why is understanding the link between the individual employee and the purpose of strategic thinking so important? All employees must be able to comprehend how their jobs support the goals, mission, and vision of their company or organization.

In simple terms, strategic thinking means knowing how to think and act creatively. It also involves teamwork, critical thinking, problem solving, and flexibility. Strategic thinkers are those who can see the big picture and understand how to achieve business goals in relation to that big picture.

You can use strategic thinking skills if you want to help develop more effective strategies to bring a business closer to its vision and goals. These include learning from feedback, making realistic predictions, streamlining the organization, and anticipating or foreseeing challenges.

The most pathetic person in the world is someone who has sight, but has no vision.
— Helen Keller

Unexpected Turbulences—What happens when you're flying along at thirty thousand feet and all of a sudden all hell breaks loose? Well, one of the reasons the pilot tells you to keep your seatbelts fastened is so that you will remain relatively safe when the unexpected turbulence occurs.

Imagine you've been flying along for a while, being a top performer at work, and suddenly the sky falls. You've hit major turbulence. It could be downsizing, a new CEO, a change in corporate philosophy, a new boss, a coworker's formal complaint, additional duties and responsibilities, or a pay cut. The list of potentials goes on and on. *You have just experienced a complete paradigm shift!* What do you do?

Well, if you are a spiritual person, you pray. Right now, you are either going through something or you are getting ready to go through something. Do not fret over things you can't control. Sacrifices must be made; after all, someone sacrificed for you.

Aside from prayer during difficult times, there is one thing you can control, and that one thing is *you*. Be still. Be patient. Be you. You may not have been issued a parachute, so bailing out is not an option. The job market will remain tough for the foreseeable future; you can't just snap your fingers and find another job. You've got to fight, use strategy, be tactful, and be smart. Make adjustments. Tough times don't last; tough people do. Put on your whole armor.

When these situations occur, and they most certainly will, you must first gain a clear understanding of the cause of the unexpected turbulence. After gaining that, you must seek a strategy to make the necessary adjustments to overcome the cause of the turbulence. After an understanding is attained and a strategy has been formulated, you must finally execute your plan. Remember, in this situation, time may not be on your side. If not, understanding, strategy, and execution must be timely.

Take your job seriously all the time, even when there is no turbulence. If you do that, you will not fear a little turbulence every once in a while. Maturity, patience, balanced thinking, confidence, and tact will get you through it.

Implementing Change— Are you afraid of change? Does change frustrate you? How do you overcome that fear or frustration? Just like employers are constantly reinventing themselves, employees also have to adapt.

The dynamics of the working environment have changed dramatically. There was a time when stability in the workplace was the norm. We have reached an era where change is the norm rather than abnormal.

In recent US history, working for the same company or organization throughout an entire career was expected. In the current environment, how often do people change careers in their lifetime? The Department of Labor indicates that collecting this kind of information "is difficult, if not impossible." But according to some labor experts, current figures range from between three and seven times.

Perhaps you can increase your odds of having career stability by putting more thought into choosing a career or deciding whether to accept a job offer. Better decision making could lead to finding a job or choosing an occupation for which you are better suited, thereby increasing the chance that you will stick with it. Of course, even taking great care when choosing a job or career doesn't mean you won't want to or need to make a change.

Those of us who are able to deal with the effects of change effectively and efficiently find ourselves in a more advantageous position than those who struggle with change. We live in a challenging and evolving work environment. Financial woes, dwindling benefits, downsizing, doing more with less, increased costs of running a business, and rising unemployment all contribute to having to implement change in the workplace. It may sound like a cliché, but change is inevitable.

The more you are able to work through nonstop changes in the workplace, the better off you will be.

Everyone thinks of changing the world, but no one thinks of changing himself.
— Leo Tolstoy

Generations and Their Characteristics

Greatest Generation (also known as the GI Generation)
Birth Years: 1901–1924
Characteristics: Team players, optimistic, respect authority, strong sense of civic obligation, frugal
Events That Shaped Life: Depression, New Deal, Roaring '20s

Silent Generation (also known as Traditionalists, Veterans, or the Mature Generation)
Birth Years: 1925–1945
Characteristics: Friendly, professional, conciliating, trust credentialed expertise
Events That Shaped Life: Depression, World War II, Korean War

Baby Boomers (also known as the Me Generation)
Birth Years: 1946–1964
Characteristics: Values orientated, idealistic, work-centric, seek self-actualization, competitive, and think they're special
Events That Shaped Life: JFK assassination, Vietnam War, civil rights movement, women's movement

Generation X
Birth Years: 1965–1980
Characteristics: Pragmatic, independent, self-reliant, individualistic, value a work-life balance, protective of their children
Events That Shaped Life: Latchkey kids, rising divorce rates

Millennial (also known as Generation Y, Next Generation, or Echo Boomers)
Birth Years: 1981–2000
Characteristics: Optimistic, civically engaged, self-confident, team orientated, close to parents, technology focused
Events That Shaped Life: 9/11, Columbine

(*USA Today*, November 18, 2010)

Critical Points of Emphasis:
The "Be Adaptable to Change" Operating System

1. To excel in this area, your ability to focus, work hard, utilize appropriate resources, plan, and prepare will help you to cope with shifting priorities.

2. Goals should be smart, measurable, attainable, relevant, trackable, or timely.

3. All employees should know how their jobs contribute to the overall success, productivity, branding, and profitability of the company or organization.

4. You must possess or learn the necessary skills to be flexible enough to handle all the challenges associated with diversity.

5. All employees must be able to comprehend how their jobs support the goals, mission, and vision of their company or organization.

6. Aside from prayer during difficult times, there is one thing you can control, and that one thing is you.

7. Take your job seriously all the time, even when there is no turbulence. If you do, you will not fear a little turbulence every once in a while.

8. Simply put, strategic thinkers are those who can see the big picture and understand how to achieve business goals in relation to that big picture.

9. Prioritizing requires that you understand timeliness and the impact of missed deadlines.

10. Prioritizing brings order to chaos.

The "Faith and Divine Authority" Operating System

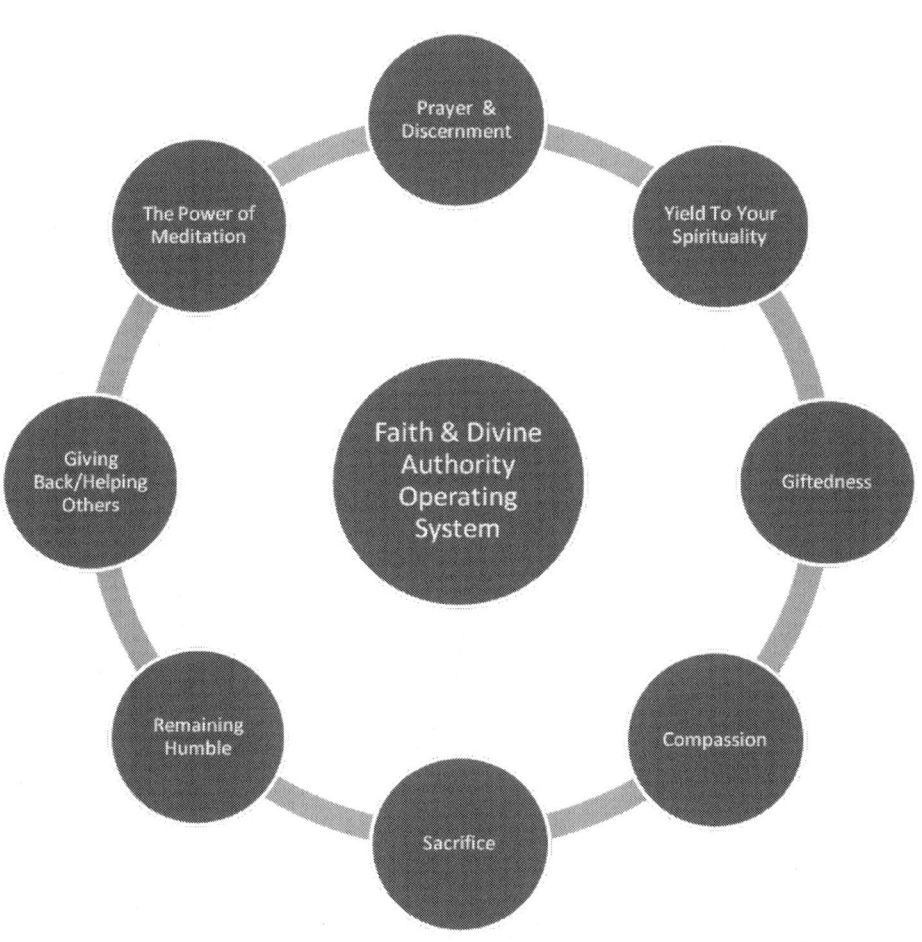

The "Faith and Divine Authority" Operating System

Being a person of faith was mentioned in the beginning, when we talked about the significance of the ten chapters. And now, in this final chapter, it is time to explore the impact of faith and recognizing divine authority. In the context that we are referring to, faith is the divinely implanted principle of inward confidence, assurance, trust, and reliance in God and all that he

> *Be on your guard; stand firm in the faith; be men of courage; be strong.*
>
> *1 Corinthians 16:13*

says. Divine authority is the recognition and acceptance that there is godly and sovereign rule over our lives.

Your faith and acknowledgement of divine authority goes a long way in determining who you are and what your outlook on life is. Why is this so important? I submit to you that before you can reap the full benefits of managing and leading yourself, you must have an understanding of who you are and who *you* are following. You should also be cognizant of divine authority over your life. Your life should exemplify whatever it is that you are attempting to impart on others.

Discussing faith and divine authority can be uncomfortable for some as well as controversial. Regardless of the feelings of discomfort and the potential controversy, without faith and recognition for divine authority, I would not be who I am today.

Endeavor to find enjoyment in your work and daily life. Hopefully, you will be able to pursue work you really enjoy and in which you can be gratified.

Yield to Your Faith and Spirituality—Life is demanding. The pressures of family are demanding. The pressures of work are *surely* demanding. Everyone is expected to do more with less; and oh, by the way, make sure you are able to come in early and leave late. If you happen to manage or supervise people, no one can ever quite pay you enough. Even working in ministry can be demanding. Extended family can also be demanding. And without a doubt, friends can be demanding. To enable you to deal with the rigors of life, inner peace is a critical attribute. A foundation of peace empowers you. When all else fails, your spirituality is unwavering.

My personal spirituality is based on Christian principles and beliefs. While confronted with different roadblocks throughout my professional career, I reached various points where I had to rely on divine intervention to overcome things that I simply did not have the power to confront alone. As I reflect on my humble beginnings, I am amazed at the power of faith and obedience. I believe that the more power and authority you possess the more in touch you need to be with your spirituality. This is especially true when leading and managing others. I have long realized that I am accountable for my actions toward and over others.

It is not always necessary for us to outwardly proclaim who we are in regard to our faith. I tend to believe that if we are who we say we are, and if we believe what we say we believe, there will always be some evidence in our character, behavior, conduct, and mannerism, along with the way we treat and interact with others.

The resistance in front of you is not greater than the force behind you.
— Pastor Terrance H. Johnson

Giftedness—We are all uniquely made. We were all placed on earth for a purpose. Each of us has a calling. But often we struggle with knowing who we are. It's sad but true that many of us go through life without knowing our purpose. But how do you know your purpose and how do you come to know who you really are? I would submit to you that the sooner you answer these questions, the more peaceful your life and work environment will be.

To some extent, the answers to the above questions can be found through studying the Word of God, prayer, meditation, counseling with an elder or mentor, and being connected with like-minded people. For those of us who are people of "faith", there are spiritual gifts assessments or analyses you can use. This is a starting place to help determine your gifts; it is not an absolute indicator.

The purpose of spiritual gifts is to build up the church and for the common good. *Some spiritual gifts are solely for the benefit of believers while others also benefit non-believers.*

In regard to your gift, my Pastor revealed the following in one of his recent messages:

- Each one of us has at least one gift
- Your gift is determined by
    - ← Evaluation – ask somebody
    - ← Experimenting – be busy; be doing something
    - ← Doing something that you are good at
- When you discover your gift, it changes your life
- Once determined, you must develop your gift
    - ← Your gift should be evident through exposure and exercise
    - ← Be in the right environment for your gift to flourish
- Deploy your gift – just do it

Do not get caught up with peer pressure, which is very easy to do. Focus on you. Accept who you are. Perfect you strengths and improve your weaknesses. I believe that your purpose in life is linked to your gifts. Once you discover them, use your purpose and gifts to enhance the lives of others and make the world a better place.

Compassion—According to history books and the Holy Bible, there was a Jewish religious teacher who lived from about 4 B.C. to A.D. 33

named Jesus. His life and teachings form the basis of Christianity. For many, including me, he provides the greatest example of compassion ever known to humankind. Compassion is kindness and consideration that cause you to refrain from damaging someone who is downtrodden or bruised. Also, compassion is described as a feeling of deep sympathy and sorrow for another who is stricken by misfortune, accompanied by a strong desire to alleviate the suffering. Practice generosity—goodness in action. Practice a caring disposition, gentleness in dealing with others, benevolence, and affability.

Showing compassion for someone in the workplace is not a sign of weakness. Where appropriate, showing compassion for another is a sign of maturity, kind-heartedness, and strength. As different things happen in the workplace, there will come a time when either you will need someone to show compassion toward you or you will need to show compassion toward someone else. Often, compassion in the workplace makes people a little squeamish, because either they feel that it is a sign of weakness or they are afraid someone will take advantage of them.

Let me assure you that there is nothing wrong with showing compassion for someone at work when appropriate. You don't have to be blind to know when someone is attempting to take advantage of you at work. There is a distinct difference between someone attempting to take advantage of you and someone not handling their duties and responsibilities.

Now, you can't show up for work late every day and expect your boss to show you compassion. But if you have small amounts of justifiable lateness, such as a couple of times per month, your boss may be understanding and is likely to show you compassion.

While working as a Hearing Officer, I often enforced regulatory policies. At the start of each session and depending upon the situation, if I could, I would tell the first offender of a particular day that I would be a little lenient, by either overlooking the offense or not giving them the full brunt of what I could have given. Jokingly, I would add that everyone who came after them was in trouble.

Remember, you are not entitled. No one is required to show you compassion. When someone does, do not take advantage of the situation. And always remember to be humble and show your gratitude toward anyone who has the heart to be compassionate.

The "Faith and Divine Authority" Operating System

Sacrifice—I learned about sacrifice at a very young age. My mother was a widow and remained one for eighteen years. Her rationale for choosing to be single for that lengthy period was that she did not want someone she really didn't know to come into her home and rule over her children. When her youngest child left home at eighteen, she remarried.

That's sacrifice. My mother worked two to three jobs to support her family. She never complained or asked for handouts. We may not have had all the material things that others had, but we were loved and happy. There are many other stories of sacrifice I could share, but this particular one stands out in my mind.

My oldest daughter is a senior in college at a state university, and my youngest daughter is attending a private university. The oldest has not had to spend one penny to help fund her education. Fortunately, my wife and I have been able to prepare wisely for this. I'm not sure if my daughters realize how truly blessed they are. I believe that each generation should be placed in a better position to succeed with their career choice, more so than prior generations. "Either make the tree good and its fruit good; or else make the tree bad and its fruit bad; for a tree is known by its fruit" (Matthew 12:33).

To be clear, the type of sacrifice I am referring to is described as a giving up of something valuable or important for somebody or something else considered of more value or importance. Even in business, the rule of sacrifice will enter your realm at some point and when it does, you will have to recognize it for what it is. For example, you may be asked to sacrifice your time without pay, and to you, the cause may or may not be a worthy one. What will you do? The company you work for could be struggling financially and ask you to forego a pay raise or even take a reduction in pay. What would you do? There is no right or wrong answer. It depends on your values, beliefs, commitment level, and internal and external circumstances.

Remaining Humble—In an earlier chapter, I talked about the army drill sergeant's efforts to motivate and help transition civilians into soldiers. Over time, a little role reversal happened, and I was placed in a position where I was responsible for motivating and transitioning others (in a somewhat different capacity). I had an eye-opening revelation: the more power you possess, the more humble you must be. I must warn you that this is contrary to what others in the workplace may think.

I discovered that I could be just as effective in achieving bottom-line results with a more humble approach. You can accomplish this by treating others with dignity, respect, honesty, integrity, and fairness. Just because you possess power and authority over others does not mean you have the right to control them. When you combine these attributes with professionalism and clear and concise communication techniques, you have a win-win combination that produces unbelievable positive results. Oh, by the way, also be willing to admit when you are wrong.

Giving Back; Helping Others—Before getting married, I was a limited giver. One thing my beautiful wife taught me was the beauty of giving back and helping others. I had to reach a certain level of maturity to understand the power associated with giving back and helping others. Hopefully, you won't have to wait as long as I did before you grasp the value of giving back and helping others.

My pastor taught me that you can't help everybody, but you can certainly help somebody. Whenever and wherever you look, there will always be somebody with a need, somebody who is less fortunate than you are. Well, the workplace is no different. There is a plethora of ways to give back and help others at work. You can offer help in the form of encouragement, support, or simply listening. Corporately, helping others builds strength in your team; loyalty is developed; and bonding will become evident. Individually helping others is simply the right thing to do, and it is gratifying knowing that you have helped to enrich the lives of others.

I always beamed with pride when someone from my staff was tapped to receive a promotion. It didn't matter whether the advancement was internal or external; the feeling of pride was the same. If no one is interested in hiring or promoting someone under your supervision, you probably are not doing enough to prepare your employees for the next level. Believe me, if you are doing your job of giving back and helping others, others notice; they hire and promote employees who demonstrate the potential for advancement.

Deep within all of us lies a philanthropist spirit. Everyone can take actions to improve the material, social, and spiritual welfare of humanity, especially through charitable activities. We can do this by helping one person at a time. This spirit can be captured through simple gestures such as mentoring, tutoring, encouraging, and volunteering.

The "Faith and Divine Authority" Operating System

The Power of Meditation—I do not have a clinical background in meditation or anything else relating to meditation, but from an everyday, practical, and spiritual approach, I have discovered the power of meditation.

In today's job environment, work is stressful; there are no two ways about it. As I engage other business professionals from various other career fields, we share a common theme of how the workplace has changed into a high-energy, do-more-with-less, increase-efficiency, and reduce-waste environment. How do you counteract the ever-present stress? One of the many ways is to meditate, to reflect. Spend some time alone with your private thoughts, your inner person, reviewing and assessing the events of the day as well as assessing yourself.

At times, sharing your thoughts and concerns with a spouse, friend, or significant other is okay, but nothing can replace the time you spend alone with your God. I believe that character and conduct begin in the mind. Your actions are affected by the things that you dwell on in your thoughts. Determine your own thought life; do not allow others to do it for you. Meditation prepares you to receive insight that you might otherwise miss.

Periodically stop and take inventory of yourself and your actions. This is one of the best self-improvement strategies you will ever invest in. The neatest thing about this self-help approach is it's free. It doesn't cost you anything.

Take a periodic inventory of your personal life so that you can enrich your mind, body, and spirit.

Prayer and Discernment—In earlier chapters, I occasionally mentioned prayer; I purposely did not elaborate in great detail on it. I took this approach because I wanted to attempt to reach all readers, believer and nonbeliever. While I was attempting not to impose my spiritual beliefs on anyone, it is important that I share my faith. It is impossible to discuss faith and divine authority without mentioning prayer, because prayer works.

Prayer was not prevalent in my life as a young man. The irony is that I grew up in a household full of prayer. As I got older, wiser, and more mature, and as I grew in my faith, prayer became and still is important to me. I challenge you not to just wait until there is a crisis in your life for you to submit yourself to prayer. Maturity is to commit to prayer at all times, without ceasing.

Prayer is communicating with God. To pray means to ask, inquire, request, desire, or wish for something from God. Prayer does not require great skill or command of any language. It is sincere, heartfelt dialogue with God the Father and Creator.

As you strive for success in the workplace, you will encounter people and situations that will render you powerless. When you do, you will discover that prayer works for you when all else fails.

If you are unsure of how to pray, seek out someone you know who would be willing to help or guide you. Admitting that you are unsure about how to pray could be the beginning of genuine and sincere prayer.

Spiritual discernment is calling on the Holy Spirit to lead or give direction in your life. While all believers are responsible for what they believe, some people are especially gifted by God for this. Men and women with the gift of discernment are specially gifted in distinguishing between those words, deeds, and appearances that are true and those that are false. Nonspiritual discernment is the ability to grasp, comprehend, and evaluate clearly. It means we can see the true nature of things; it allows us to distinguish between what is real and what is imitation.

According to Joe Contaldi Ministries, discernment is sound judgment which enables us to do the following?

- Understand the times and significance of world events and events in our own lives.
- See beyond outward facades or appearances to the heart of the matter or to the heart of a person.
- Distinguish between what is good and what is evil.
- Recognize God's ways, his deeds and actions for his people.
- Comprehend spiritual realities and spiritual truths.
- Establish God's righteous government on the earth, affirming Jesus's legal right to reign and rule as King of kings and Lord of lords.
- Avoid the schemes of the enemy, and therefore, avoid life's pitfalls.
- Make wise and godly decisions, both on a personal and on a community level.

Discernment is part of our transformation into maturity as our minds are renewed.

Addendum to the "Faith and Divine Authority" Operating System

Flying Instrument Flight Rules (**IFR**)

Or, Is Faith Real?

In aviation, the pilot has two methods of flying and filing a flight plan: Instrument Flight Rules (IFR) and Visual Flight Rules (VFR).

During flight under IFR, there are no visibility requirements, so flying through clouds (or other conditions where there is zero visibility outside the aircraft) is legal and safe. Because IFR flights often take place without visual reference to the ground, a means of navigation other than looking outside the window is required. IFR pilots must meticulously evaluate weather, create a very detailed flight plan based around specific instrument departure, en route and arrival procedures, and dispatch the flight. For further edification, when flying IFR, pilots must rely solely on what their instruments inside the cockpit reveal to them while taking off, during flight, and landing the aircraft.

VFR flights are much simpler than IFR and require significantly less training and practice. VFR provides a great degree of freedom, allowing pilots to go where they want, when they want, and allowing them much wider latitude in determining how they get there. During VFR, you're still flying along just like IFR, except you can see where you are going. Should your visibility become limited during VFR, you've got a serious problem.

Like VFR flights, not fearing God or lacking faith may allow you to feel as if you have a greater degree of freedom. Likewise, not fearing God or lacking faith may also mislead you into believing that you have a wider latitude in living your life any way you want to, without restrictions or consequences.

Flying IFR is similar to your faith: you can't touch it, you can't see it, but you just know and believe it's there, guiding you through adverse situations. During IFR flight, you must rely on your IFR training just as you must rely on your faith, knowledge, and understanding of the Word of God. The pilot must have complete faith in whatever his or her instruments are revealing, regardless of what he or she feels or thinks. This is what your faith is like. You believe. You trust. You have confidence in God and his Word. You may experience some uneasiness because you cannot always see where your faith is leading you, but you have the comfort of knowing that, wherever the destination, you are bound to arrive there safely.

Critical Points of Emphasis:
The "Faith and Divine Authority" Operating System

1. To enable you to deal with the rigors of life, inner peace is a critical attribute. A foundation of peace empowers you.

2. While confronted with different roadblocks throughout my professional career, I have reached various points when I had to rely on divine intervention to overcome things that I simply did not have the power to confront alone.

3. I believe that the more power and authority you possess, the more in touch you need to be with your spirituality

4. Determine your own thought life; do not allow others to do it for you.

5. How well or poorly you prioritize the different needs in your life will affect almost everything you do and every decision you make.

6. Prayer is sincere, heartfelt dialogue with God the Father and Creator.

7. Your life should exemplify whatever it is that you are attempting to impart to others.

8. Focus on you. Accept who you are. Perfect your strength and improve your weaknesses.

9. The more power you possess, the more humble you must be.

10. Individually giving back and helping others is simply the right thing to do, and it is gratifying knowing that you have helped to enrich the lives of others.

11. Take a periodic inventory of your personal life so that you can enrich your mind, body, and spirit.

12. If we are who we say we are and if we believe what we say we believe, there will always be some evidence in our character, behavior, conduct, and mannerism, along with the way we treat and interact with others.

13. Not Fearing God or lacking faith may mislead you into believing that you have a wider latitude in living your life any way you want to, without restrictions or consequences.

Bonus Module
A Snippet on Leadership

Those with a passion for leadership have created many definitions of it, and there are common points in all the definitions. Through my own research, I submit that this is the best description of leadership: "Leadership is about influencing others toward achieving a common goal."

Control is not leadership; management is not leadership; leadership is leadership. If you seek to lead, invest at least 50% of your time in leading yourself—your own purpose, ethics, principles, motivation, conduct. Invest at least 20% leading those with authority over you and 15% leading your peers.
— Dee Hock

The key to successful leadership today is influence, not authority.
— Kenneth Blanchard

The biggest difference is that managers get the most out of themselves; leaders get the most out of others.
— Dr. Samuel Chand

To be successful, study success. People who are or have been successful have so much to offer. Allow me to dream for a moment. If I could, I would assemble my own business dream team. I would sit down at a huge conference table and make myself like a sponge. I would absorb everything I could. Since this is not possible, the next best thing is to find and read select publications about powerful and influential leaders. My dream team of leaders who can be celebrated as example for others to emulate include the following:

- Courage—Abe Lincoln, US president
- Innovation and technology—Bill Gates, former chairman of Microsoft, American businessman, philanthropist
- Leadership—Colin Powell, American statesman, retired four- star general
- Motivation, focus, and ambition—Oprah Winfrey, entertainer and philanthropist
- Passion—Vince Lombardi, former professional football coach
- Perseverance—Nelson Mandela, former president, South Africa
- Sacrifice—Muhammad Ali, retired professional boxer
- Spiritual influence—Dr. Samuel Chand, leadership architect and change strategist, and Pastor Terrance H. Johnson, pastor and founder, Higher Dimension Church
- Teamwork—the thirty-three Chilean miners rescued from the San Jose Mine in northern Chile in October 2010.
- Thinking outside the box—Herbert D. Kelleher, cofounder, chairman emeritus, former CEO of Southwest Airlines
- Vision—Dr. Martin Luther King Jr., civil rights leader

Leadership Axioms

- Credibility is essential to leadership.
- Earning respect from others is critical to leadership; there is a distinct difference between earning respect and being given respect. Positional power and authority must be given respect, but this does not mean that the person with the positional power and authority has actually earned their due respect.
- In leadership, do not say one thing and do another.

Bonus Module A Snippet on Leadership

- Leaders are always in control of themselves and the situation.
- Leaders are problem solvers.
- Leaders are self-motivated.
- Leaders are unafraid to empower others.
- Leaders are visionaries.
- Leaders deflect credit to others and assume blame for the failures of others.
- Leaders display courage at times when others are hesitant.
- Leaders do not become unraveled in pressure situations.
- Leaders do not compromise their integrity.
- Leaders know they do not know everything.
- Leaders lead others the way they would want to be led.
- Leaders listen.
- Leaders place the welfare of their company or organization and the employees above their personal ambitions.
- Leaders understand delegation and accountability.
- Leadership and discernment are cohabitants.
- Leadership is lonely.
- Leadership is not people pleasing.
- Leadership is not for everyone.
- Leadership, accountability, and responsibility are synonymous.
- The best leaders are great communicators.

That's a Wrap

We began this journey with the "Develop Self-Discipline" operating system, and we conclude with the "Faith and Divine Authority" operating system. I view these two chapters as bookends. Like bookends, self-discipline and faith and divine authority will keep you upright while also providing support for other materials inside of the bookends.

During your professional journey, you will encounter some people and situations that you never anticipated. When this happens, you will find yourself relying on your acquired knowledge, skills, training, and resources to help get you through. At the end of the day, if you have the self-assurance that you did your best, that you treated everyone the way you would want others to treat you, then all should be right with you.

I have benefitted immensely from this project. In fact, this undertaking was therapeutic for me. While working on this project, I had to take a small sabbatical. This time off was needed because of the loss of my dear mother. I needed a little time to regroup.

Working on this project had its highs and lows (as does anything in life). It was simply exhilarating to watch this creative piece come together before my eyes. It is my hope and prayer that your life has been positively affected and enriched by something that was said. Through it all, God has been good to me.

Be blessed.

C.E. Dickens

About the Author

Calvin Dickens has been leading and managing people for thirty-three-plus years, during which he has had many successes and some failures. Calvin's chosen career field has enabled him to live and work in numerous places around the world. He has also had the privilege of working side by side with and for men and women from various ethnic, religious, educational, and socioeconomic backgrounds.

The author has been fortunate to experience the intricacies of leadership and workplace performance and productivity at a major airport system (multiple airports under one umbrella). Calvin has firsthand experience with numerous leadership and business processes, such as Blanchard, Model-Netics, Balanced Score Card, High Performance Organization, and DISC Development.

Calvin is a certified aircraft dispatcher. He has worked as a flight operations coordinator, supervisor, and chief. In this capacity, he learned many things that were beneficial to developing his administrative, planning, and organizational skills. This work also placed Calvin at the epicenter of his companies' and organizations' operational nerve centers.

The author has also had a lifelong fascination with leadership. This fascination intensified during his twenty-year U.S. Army career. Calvin believes there are many facets of military leadership that have withstood the test of time. The leadership traits and attributes he learned were life changing. Leadership was also displayed through sports management. Calvin worked as a certified International Association of Approved Basketball Officials referee, a certified Amateur Boxing Federation referee and judge, and a certified Amateur Softball Association umpire.

Calvin has served or is currently serving on several boards of directors, extending across four very different businesses and professional interests. These opportunities include or included serving on the board for a large faith-based organization, a sports officials' association, a property investment group, and a large property-management company. Calvin has also been fortunate to have been placed in several pivotal support positions during such mega-events as the 1988 Summer Olympics and Super Bowl XXXVIII.

Calvin has been married to his lovely wife, a professional, independent, and God-fearing woman, for twenty-eight years. He is also very proud of his daughters; the oldest is a college senior and his youngest is a college freshman.

Resources

7 Ways to Improve Employee Morale by Michael F. McDougall
Earl Carl Institute for Legal and Social Policy, Inc.
http://www.buzzle.com/articles/professionalism-in-the-workplace.html
http://www.leadership-with-you.com/characteristics-of-a-good-team.html
http://www.ridingthebeast.com/numbers/nu10.php
http://www.webopedia.com/TERM/O/operating_system.html
Joe Contaldi Ministries
Management Essentials for Christian Ministries
Model-Netics
National Center for Education Statistics
Swiss Army Knife
The Condition of Education, 2010
The National Labor Relations Act
The Spirit-Filled Bible, King James Version
U.S. Department of Commerce, Census Bureau, Current Population Survey (CPS), Annual Social and Economic Supplement, 2011

U.S. Department of Education
USA Today, November 18, 2010
www.victorsafety.com
Wallpaper5.com

Made in the USA
Columbia, SC
12 June 2018